START
HERE

BIG
QUESTIONS

Where?

LONDON, NEW YORK,
MELBOURNE, MUNICH, AND DELHI

SENIOR EDITOR ANDREA MILLS
SENIOR ART EDITOR JACQUI SWAN
MANAGING EDITOR LINDA ESPOSITO
MANAGING ART EDITOR JIM GREEN

CATEGORY PUBLISHER LAURA BULLER
DESIGN DEVELOPMENT MANAGER SOPHIA M. TAMPAKOPOULOS TURNER
SENIOR PRODUCTION CONTROLLER ANGELA GRAEF
PRODUCTION EDITOR SIU CHAN
JACKET EDITOR MATILDA GOLLON
JACKET DESIGNER JACQUI SWAN

WRITTEN BY LAURA BULLER, SUSAN KENNEDY, ANDREA MILLS
SPACE CONSULTANCY CAROLE STOTT

ILLUSTRATIONS BY TADO

First published in the United States in 2011
by DK Publishing
375 Hudson Street, New York, New York 10014

A Penguin Company

Copyright © 2011 Dorling Kindersley Limited

2 4 6 8 10 9 7 5 3 1
180633–13/12

A catalog record for this book is available from the Library of Congress.

ISBN 978-0-7566-7579-0

High-res workflow proofed by Media Development Printing Ltd., U.K.
Printed and bound by Toppan, China

Discover more at
www.dk.com

Why?

How?

CONTENTS

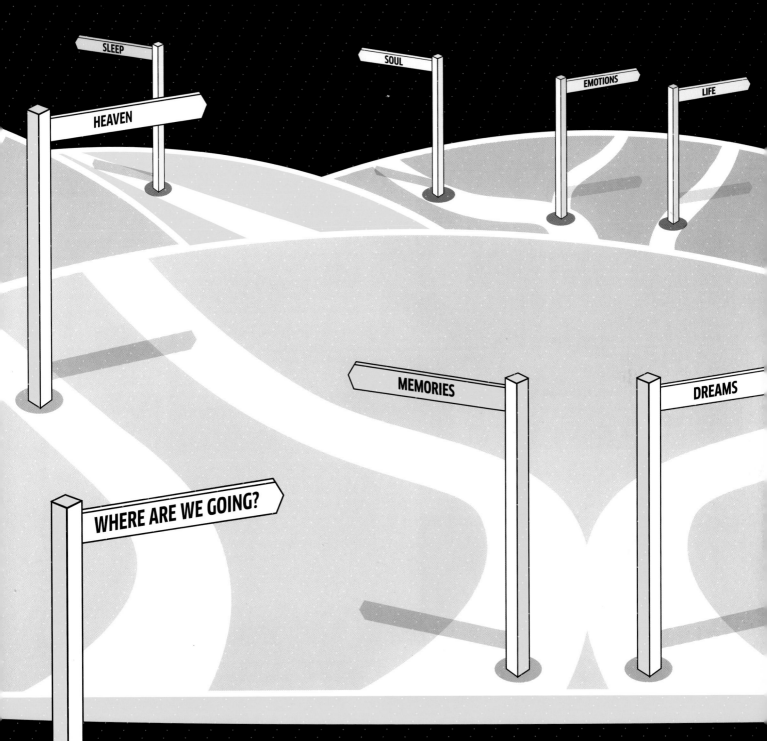

"WOULD YOU TELL ME, PLEASE, WHICH WAY I OUGHT TO GO FROM HERE?"
"THAT DEPENDS A GOOD DEAL ON WHERE YOU WANT TO GET TO," SAID THE CAT.
"I DON'T MUCH CARE WHERE," SAID ALICE.
"THEN IT DOESN'T MATTER WHICH WAY YOU GO," SAID THE CAT.
"SO LONG AS I GET SOMEWHERE," ALICE ADDED AS AN EXPLANATION.
"OH, YOU'RE SURE TO DO THAT," SAID THE CAT, "IF YOU ONLY WALK LONG ENOUGH."

Lewis Carroll, from *Alice's Adventures in Wonderland*

WHY ARE YOU READING THIS?

Only you can answer this question, of course. It could be for any number of reasons. Perhaps you have nothing else to do and the book fell open at this page or you're a real bookworm, determined to read this from cover to cover. A more general answer is that you are reading it to gain knowledge from the words written on the page. Keep on reading to discover more about knowledge and why you need it.

SHHH! READING IN PROGRESS

"THERE IS MUCH PLEASURE TO BE GAINED FROM USELESS KNOWLEGE."
Bertrand Russell (1872-1970), British philosopher

READING MATTERS
The most common way to get knowledge is by reading, whether it is an encyclopedia of reference facts or an adventure story of drama and excitement. Printed words are everywhere you look—on food labels, street signs, and the Internet. You spend many more minutes a day reading than you realize, and all of this reading tops off your memory stores with knowledge.

TRUE OR FALSE?
People don't always tell the truth, so ask yourself a few questions before you take someone's knowledge to be true. Has that person ever lied before? Can they back up their facts with evidence? Do other people accept their ideas as true? These tests work for knowledge gained from both books and people.

WHAT IS KNOWLEDGE?
Knowledge is what you learn about the world from your experiences and from other people. Your sense organs are constantly sending information to the brain. A tiny proportion is retained and stored in the brain as long-term memory—or knowledge.

SURVIVAL SKILLS
If you didn't have knowledge, you would still be as helpless as a baby and unable to take care of yourself. You need to know hundreds and thousands of things just to stay alive—that you have to eat every day, that hot things burn, that cars are dangerous—the list is endless. Without this knowledge, you wouldn't last very long at all.

WAY TO THE TOP
Knowledge is power. It will help in everything you set out to do. Building up a large base of knowledge will keep you ahead of the competition. Who knows? You may even end up running the country or winning a Nobel Prize. You're already on the way; as American physician Benjamin Spock (1903–1998) said, "You know more than you think you do."

FUN FACTOR
Natural curiosity makes us want to find out about the world around us and how it works. Learning more information means you can take part in quizzes and win prizes for your general knowledge. You can also impress your friends with different skills, such as soccer. You couldn't score a goal without first knowing how to kick a ball.

CAN YOU DISCOVER KNOWLEDGE?
Knowledge is not just something you get from reading books or listening to teachers. The discoveries you make for yourself are even more important, and you make them all the time without always recognizing it. Here are three ways you find things out for yourself, but there are many other ways, too.

TRIAL AND ERROR
This is a way of gathering information by testing various ideas and seeing which one will work the best. For example, to make a paper airplane, you construct several prototypes (trial models) and test-fly them until you come up with the perfect design.

OBSERVATION
One of the most important ways we learn is by watching other people do things and then imitating them. When you see other people sit down on chairs, you understand their purpose and learn to sit on a chair for yourself. This is the power of observation.

MAKING MISTAKES
You discover that some actions lead to unpleasant consequences and remember to avoid them. This is also called learning from experience. That person has learned the hard way to check whether his chair is safe to sit on. In the future, he won't make the same mistake again.

WHERE DID THE UNIVERSE COME FROM?

BANG! That's how the universe started. A huge explosion, now known as the big bang, marked the beginning of everything, about 13.7 billion years ago. Scientists believe that in that moment, the entire universe, including time and space, got under way. It was even smaller than a period back then and was made up of miniscule particles of energy. It's difficult to comprehend, and even scientists don't know exactly why the big bang occurred, but they agree that this is where the universe had its beginning.

ALL ROUTES

UNIVERSAL DEVELOPMENT

It may seem like the universe is made up of all sorts of things, but everything that exists is either matter or energy. Objects, air, and water are examples of matter. Most of the matter in the universe has joined to form stars, which exist in groups called galaxies. Sound, light, heat, and motion are examples of energy. The universe started out small, dense, and hot. Over time, it has been expanding, changing, and cooling to form the universe today.

EXPERT THEORIES

In 1931, Belgian astronomer Georges Lemaître suggested that an explosion gave birth to the universe. The name "big bang" came from English astronomer Fred Hoyle, who was ridiculing the theory in 1949. Despite this, the name stuck. Today, experts know that the big bang occurred because energy from the explosion still fills the universe. Called cosmic microwave background radiation, the energy is mapped by satellites above Earth.

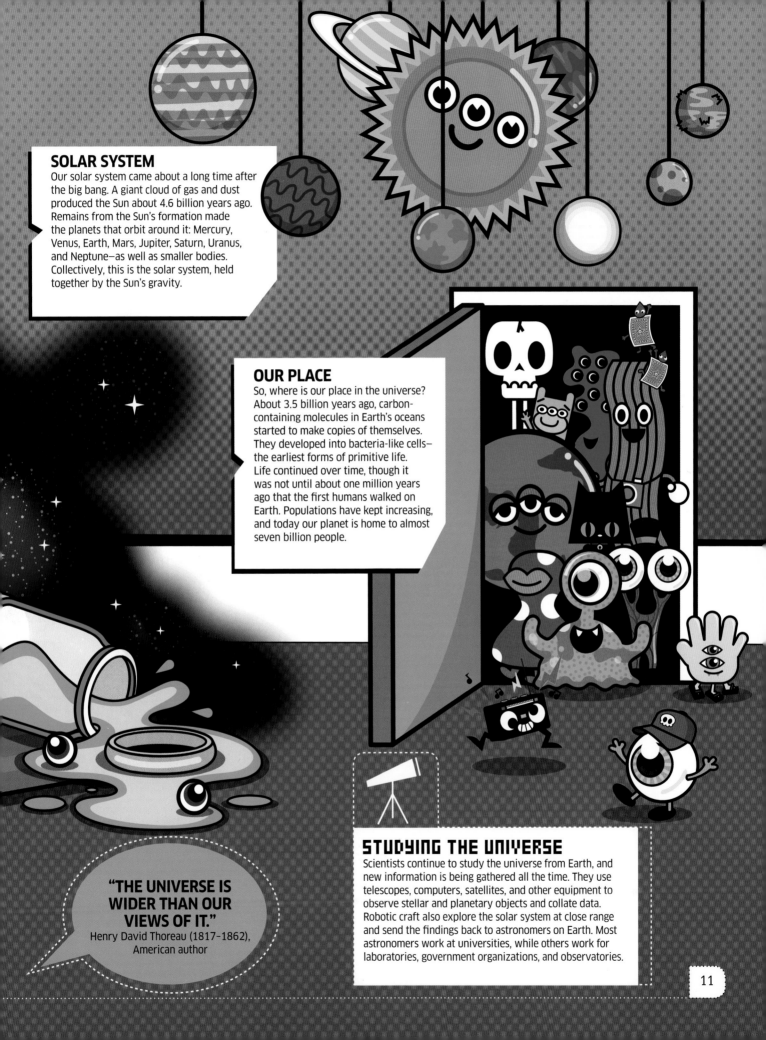

SOLAR SYSTEM

Our solar system came about a long time after the big bang. A giant cloud of gas and dust produced the Sun about 4.6 billion years ago. Remains from the Sun's formation made the planets that orbit around it: Mercury, Venus, Earth, Mars, Jupiter, Saturn, Uranus, and Neptune—as well as smaller bodies. Collectively, this is the solar system, held together by the Sun's gravity.

OUR PLACE

So, where is our place in the universe? About 3.5 billion years ago, carbon-containing molecules in Earth's oceans started to make copies of themselves. They developed into bacteria-like cells—the earliest forms of primitive life. Life continued over time, though it was not until about one million years ago that the first humans walked on Earth. Populations have kept increasing, and today our planet is home to almost seven billion people.

STUDYING THE UNIVERSE

Scientists continue to study the universe from Earth, and new information is being gathered all the time. They use telescopes, computers, satellites, and other equipment to observe stellar and planetary objects and collate data. Robotic craft also explore the solar system at close range and send the findings back to astronomers on Earth. Most astronomers work at universities, while others work for laboratories, government organizations, and observatories.

"THE UNIVERSE IS WIDER THAN OUR VIEWS OF IT."
Henry David Thoreau (1817–1862), American author

WHAT'S THE MATTER WITH MATTER?

In the first moments after the big bang, tiny particles of energy from the explosion converted into particles of matter—the substance of which things are made. Much later, when the universe was about 300,000 years old, the first atoms began to form from this matter. Made of hydrogen and helium gas, these atoms went on to create the other chemical elements that exist today. Earth and eventually everything on it came from these elements, yet they make up less than five per cent of the universe. With only a tiny part accounted for, it wasn't the end of the matter...

MYSTERIOUS UNIVERSE

The other 96 percent of the universe is something of a mystery. It appears that it is made up of two types of hidden substances—unknown matter called dark matter and a mysterious force called dark energy. Although it is not possible to directly detect them, scientists believe they exist because of their effect on objects that we can see.

DARK FORCES

The invisible dark matter does not release any detectable energy, but its gravity has an effect on its surroundings. Let's start in space, where galaxies are arranged in clusters. Although these galaxies are visible to astronomers, there are movements of galaxies within clusters that can be explained only by the gravity of an unseen material pulling on them as they move in the universe. Known as dark matter, this material makes up about 23 percent of the entire universe. Do the math—that's 27 percent explained. So, what about the rest? A whopping 73 percent of the universe is believed to be an unknown form of energy. In 1998, astronomers studying supernovae (exploding stars) showed how they could be used to determine the speed of the universe's expansion. It was thought that the expansion rate was slowing down, but the supernovae suggested it was actually speeding up. Astronomers discovered a repulsive force pushing the universe apart that modifies the gravity of ordinary matter pulling it together. Enter dark energy. While the gravitational force of dark matter helps pull the universe together, the repulsive force of dark energy makes the universe expand more rapidly.

MATTER OF FACT

Theories are being developed all the time that attempt to offer a different version of the universe with different, or no, roles for dark matter and dark energy. However, many of these theories have been overturned by scientists. New ideas are usually dismissed, as they do not stand up to further research and investigation. Dark matter and dark energy remain the accepted explanations, no matter what.

HOW CAN THE UNIVERSE BE INFINITE?

It is difficult to imagine something going on forever. That is why ancient astronomers believed that, somewhere far beyond the stars, there was an end to the universe. They thought there must be an edge marking where the universe ceased to be. Now we know that, however far and fast you travel through the universe, you would never reach an end. Some theories of the universe suggest that it has only a limited volume, which means that you might return to your starting point if you traveled long enough.

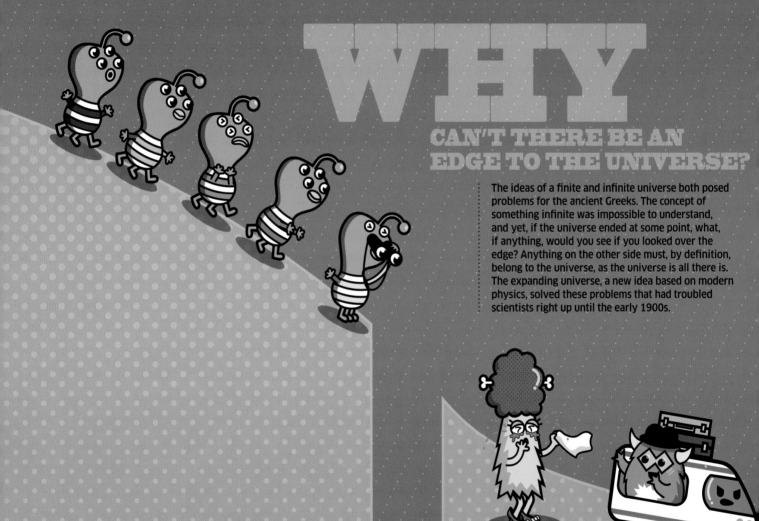

WHY CAN'T THERE BE AN EDGE TO THE UNIVERSE?

The ideas of a finite and infinite universe both posed problems for the ancient Greeks. The concept of something infinite was impossible to understand, and yet, if the universe ended at some point, what, if anything, would you see if you looked over the edge? Anything on the other side must, by definition, belong to the universe, as the universe is all there is. The expanding universe, a new idea based on modern physics, solved these problems that had troubled scientists right up until the early 1900s.

IF: THE UNIVERSE IS ALL THERE IS, HOW CAN IT EXPAND?

When a glowing object moves away from us, its light is known to become redder than usual. Measurements of galaxy clusters show that their light is reddened, so they must be moving away. The universe has been expanding since the big bang. This is not because extra matter is appearing but because galaxy clusters are getting farther apart. Maybe there is extra room in the universe if there is space for galaxies to spread farther apart, but exactly how much room is left we do not know. The universe cannot be expanding into anything other than itself, for whatever it is expanding into is part of the universe, as there is nothing other than the universe.

WHICH BRIGHT SPARK FIGURED OUT THAT THE UNIVERSE IS EXPANDING?

In the 1910s, American astronomer Vesto Slipher discovered that the light from some galaxies was redder than others. By the 1920s, American astronomer Edwin Hubble had found a way to measure the distances of galaxies, so he and fellow astronomer Milton Humason compared the levels of reddening with these distances. They discovered that the more distant galaxies were moving away faster, which suggested that the universe was expanding.

WHAT SIZE IS THE UNIVERSE TODAY?

Measuring units, such as miles and kilometers, are regularly used on Earth, but they are too small to describe the mind-boggling distances beyond the solar system. Light travels at an amazing 186,282 miles (299,792 km) per second. A light-year is the distance that light travels in one year–about 6 trillion miles (10 trillion km). The detectable universe is at least 90 billion light-years across. Nothing moves faster than light, but distances in the universe are so great that it can take years for the light to reach us.

HOW WILL THE UNIVERSE END?

Scientists think the universe will end in one of three ways–either the galaxies, stars, and atoms in the universe will eventually rip themselves apart or the universe will expand forever, gradually cooling until it is completely dark and dead. It is also possible that the universe will stop expanding and crash in on itself. These three theories are called the big rip, big chill, and big crunch.

THE END

HOW DO WE KNOW THAT DINOSAURS EVEN EXISTED?

A long time ago, Earth was a monsters' world. With gigantic jaws and scaly skins, this group of creatures called dinosaurs dominated the planet for 160 million years. It may sound far-fetched, but proof of their existence is still with us today. Scientists have found the fossilized bones of dinosaurs and sometimes whole skeletons. These remains give an intriguing insight to ancient life and provide clear evidence that early examples of life were very different to those found today.

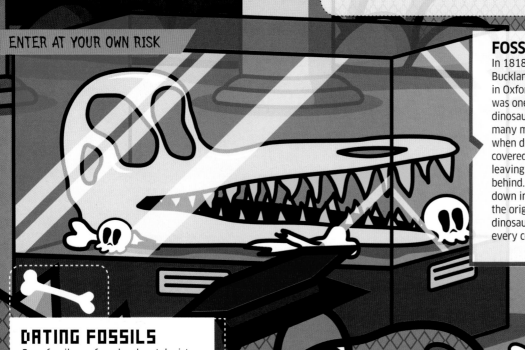

ENTER AT YOUR OWN RISK

FOSSIL FINDS

In 1818, British geologist William Buckland discovered a giant fossilized jaw in Oxfordshire, England. This exciting find was one of the first-known discoveries of dinosaur remains. By the end of the 1800s, many more fossils were found. They formed when dinosaurs died and were quickly covered by mud. Soft body parts rotted, leaving only bones and other hard parts behind. In time, these hard parts broke down into minerals, leaving rocky copies of the originals. Evidence for the existence of dinosaurs has now been discovered on every continent.

DATING FOSSILS

Once fossils are found, paleontologists (scientists who study fossils) determine their approximate age using a method called radiometric dating. Fossils form in layers of rock that can be dated, with each layer older than the one above. Radiometric dating is reliable because it agrees with other dating methods, such as geology and astronomical observations of Earth's rotation. By dating fossils, an accurate timeline of evolution is compiled.

DINOSAUR LIVING

Fossils help paleontologists reconstruct what dinosaurs looked like, how they moved, and what they ate. Sharp teeth and claws suggest that a dinosaur ate meat. This type of dinosaur was bipedal (two-footed), which enabled it to quickly chase prey. Plant-eating dinosaurs were usually quadrupeds (four-footed), with teeth suited to grinding vegetation. Fossilized footprints indicate dinosaur weight and confirm that they traveled in groups, with the young in the middle to protect them.

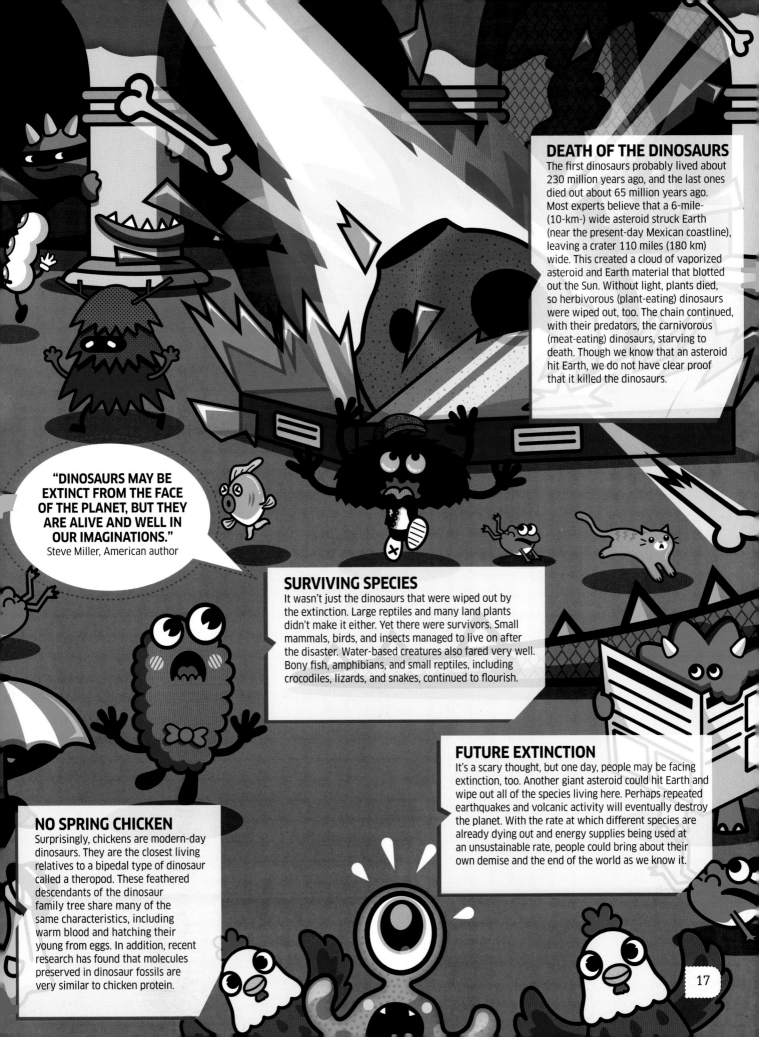

DEATH OF THE DINOSAURS

The first dinosaurs probably lived about 230 million years ago, and the last ones died out about 65 million years ago. Most experts believe that a 6-mile- (10-km-) wide asteroid struck Earth (near the present-day Mexican coastline), leaving a crater 110 miles (180 km) wide. This created a cloud of vaporized asteroid and Earth material that blotted out the Sun. Without light, plants died, so herbivorous (plant-eating) dinosaurs were wiped out, too. The chain continued, with their predators, the carnivorous (meat-eating) dinosaurs, starving to death. Though we know that an asteroid hit Earth, we do not have clear proof that it killed the dinosaurs.

"DINOSAURS MAY BE EXTINCT FROM THE FACE OF THE PLANET, BUT THEY ARE ALIVE AND WELL IN OUR IMAGINATIONS."
Steve Miller, American author

SURVIVING SPECIES

It wasn't just the dinosaurs that were wiped out by the extinction. Large reptiles and many land plants didn't make it either. Yet there were survivors. Small mammals, birds, and insects managed to live on after the disaster. Water-based creatures also fared very well. Bony fish, amphibians, and small reptiles, including crocodiles, lizards, and snakes, continued to flourish.

FUTURE EXTINCTION

It's a scary thought, but one day, people may be facing extinction, too. Another giant asteroid could hit Earth and wipe out all of the species living here. Perhaps repeated earthquakes and volcanic activity will eventually destroy the planet. With the rate at which different species are already dying out and energy supplies being used at an unsustainable rate, people could bring about their own demise and the end of the world as we know it.

NO SPRING CHICKEN

Surprisingly, chickens are modern-day dinosaurs. They are the closest living relatives to a bipedal type of dinosaur called a theropod. These feathered descendants of the dinosaur family tree share many of the same characteristics, including warm blood and hatching their young from eggs. In addition, recent research has found that molecules preserved in dinosaur fossils are very similar to chicken protein.

CAN WE KNOW ANYTHING FOR SURE?

You can be sure about things you have experienced for yourself. For example, you know that water is wet and that fire burns. You know what you had for breakfast (things in the past) and what you are wearing (things in the present), though you cannot be sure about the future. You also "know" far more things than your own experience tells you—information you get from other people, such as parents and teachers. But can you be sure it's true?

KNOWING AND BELIEVING

There is a difference between what we know for a fact to be true and what we believe to be true. Factual knowledge is based on eyewitness evidence (either our own or that of other people), rational explanation, and scientific proof. Belief is based on the hope or confidence that something is true. People of all religious faiths have no doubt that their beliefs are the truth, but they cannot prove for certain that God or the supernatural exists.

SURE THING

One thing is guaranteed, and we all have to face it—one day we are going to die. Actually, according to American statesman and scientist Benjamin Franklin (1706–1790), there are only two guarantees—death and taxes.

COMMON KNOWLEDGE

We possess a vast database of information that has been built up over generations of human existence. It is passed on in the stories parents tell their children, the books authors write, and the records people leave behind them. More and more of this information is being stored on the Internet. It is always growing and changing as people make new discoveries that alter our ideas about the past or reveal new facts about the world and the universe. Today, we know for a certainty that Earth and the other planets orbit the Sun, but for thousands of years, people believed the exact opposite— that the Sun circles around Earth. After all, both Greek philosopher Aristotle (384–322 BCE), the greatest authority of the ancient world, and the Bible, the Christian holy book, said so, and they couldn't be wrong, could they?

BACK TO SCHOOL

Well, yes they could. About 400 years ago, astronomers proved beyond a mathematical doubt that Earth goes around the Sun. They were persecuted because they opposed the Christian Church's teachings and upset "accepted" knowledge. But they paved the way for a series of revolutionary discoveries of modern science. For example, astronomy, physics, and medicine—that laid the foundations of four humors. That was another idea the scientific body was made up of four humors. That was another idea the scientific At one time doctors believed that they had too much blood. (black bile, yellow bile, phlegm, and blood). Phew—some of those old cures were scary! revolution helped lay to rest. Phew—some of those old cures were scary! when people turned red in the sun, it was believed that they had too much blood. Bloodletting (when you purposely cut yourself) was practiced to balance their humors.

NEW DISCOVERIES

Don't try to predict the future. In 1900, Lord William Kelvin, a leading British physicist, said, "There is nothing new to be discovered in physics now." Only five years later, Albert Einstein published his groundbreaking "theory of relativity," which changed physics forever. Here are just a few things that no one knew about at the beginning of the 1900s: particle physics, nuclear energy, plate tectonics, space exploration, and black holes. These discoveries have fundamentally changed our knowledge of the universe. Can you imagine life without televisions, computers, antibiotics, lasers, and the Internet? Yet none of these had been invented then. One thing is for sure—there will always be something new to discover.

FLAWED SCIENCE

Scientists are human, just like the rest of us, and this means they sometimes make mistakes. Before they announce a new discovery to the world, they normally present their findings to a team of fellow scientists, who closely scrutinize them. This process is called "peer review" and helps eliminate errors. Even so, scientists often disagree with one another, and this can make it difficult for nonscientists to know exactly what to believe. For example, climate scientists agree that the average surface temperature of Earth has risen, but they have offered a variety of different explanations for the causes of this global warming. While some scientists believe that global warming is caused by human pollution, others blame the natural cycle of Earth warming up and cooling down from the Sun's activity.

UNSOLVED MYSTERIES

Ancient peoples believed that Earth was supported on the back of a giant turtle standing on four elephants. That may sound crazy to us, but we can be sure that many ideas we now accept as scientific "truth" will seem just as absurd to future generations. Researchers at the CERN Large Hadron Collider deep under the ground in Switzerland hope that their experiments will throw light on the big bang that brought the universe into being. This is only one of hundreds of mysteries that science has yet to solve.

WHERE
DO WE COME FROM?

Throughout history, people have given very different explanations for how living things first appeared on Earth. The big debate continues as to whether life has evolved over time or whether life was created by a god. Those who look to science for the answer claim that species have evolved over time. By contrast, some people of a religious faith believe that their god created the universe and all of the life within it. Some people believe in a combination of these two theories.

EVOLUTIONARY PROCESS
Today, almost all of the world's scientists agree about how life appeared on Earth. They claim that the variety of different species developed gradually, over many millions of years, in a process called evolution. Initially, there were only very simple life forms, but as they reproduced, they altered and adapted slightly. Over huge periods of time, these changes became bigger until entirely new and more complicated types

of life forms emerged. British naturalist Charles Darwin (1809–1882) explained the way in which species evolve with his theory of "natural selection." He stated that simple structures, such as bacteria, can become complex organisms by adapting well to their environments. Not all plants and animals survive, because of predators, disease, or lack of food. Those that adapt by growing a furry winter coat or developing strong eyesight to avoid predators, for example, will be more likely to find a partner and mate. Their offspring inherit these adaptations, increasing their chance of survival.

EARTH'S TIMELINE
The evolutionary timeline starts 3.5 billion years ago, when carbon-containing molecules evolved into basic bacteria-like cells. About 450 million years ago, water-based life started to move onto land and develop into reptiles. The dinosaurs burst onto the scene about 230 million years ago, with the last ones dying out about 65 million years ago. Approximately five million years later, it was the turn of primates—the group of mammals

to which humans belong. However, humans are a young species compared to many primates and evolved about one million years ago. We're positively youthful in the grand scheme of things.

GOD'S GIFT
Creationism is the belief that the universe and all life forms were created by a god or gods. The first book of Christianity, Genesis, states that the universe was created in about 4000 BCE. Some religious enthusiasts agree, insisting that evolution cannot explain the rich diversity of life on Earth, but the special powers of a god can. While scientists believe that the universe is 13.7 billion years old, Christian creationists believe that it is only 6,000 years old. However, does a belief in evolution have to cancel out a belief that a god created the universe? Some people argue that God could have created the big bang and then instigated evolution. This allows the theories of creationism and evolution to exist side by side.

WHAT IS THE MEANING OF LIFE?

This is surely the biggest question of all, and people have been asking themselves it throughout history. Why are we here on this tiny planet called Earth in the vast immensity of the universe? Have we been put here for a purpose? Do our lives have any value or significance? Where are we all going? This game takes you on a path to discover what might be the true meaning of life, and it's your move first . . .

IN THE LIFELINE

FAMILY BASE
The most important thing in life is being there for your nearest and dearest—grandparents, parents, siblings, and children. Most of us would put our families first. For Chinese people, "filial piety" (respect for elder family members) is among the greatest of virtues. It is owed to the living and the dead, including distant ancestors.

GENETIC JUNCTION
The primary reason that all living things exist is to replicate their DNA and ensure the survival of their genes. The human species is no different from any other species in this respect. Everyone alive on Earth today is descended from a common ancestor who lived in Africa more than 150,000 years ago.

HEAVENLY DESIGN
The universe is too complex to have come about by accident. Only a supernatural intelligence (God) could have created it and designed Earth with the right physical conditions (oxygen, food, water) to support life. Humans are part of God's creation and are here to carry out God's purposes.

SPIRITUAL CYCLE
According to many Eastern religions, such as Hinduism and Buddhism, human existence is an ever-repeating cycle of birth, death, and rebirth. After the body dies, the soul, or spirit, returns to Earth in a new body. Each soul passes through a succession of lifetimes on its cosmic journey.

TALENT ON TRACK
What gives meaning and value to life is aiming to be the best at whatever you do, whether it is being a doctor, musician, cleaner, or just Blob. We are all good at something, and it's a question of finding out where your skills and talents lie and then developing them. Basically, life is what you choose to make of it.

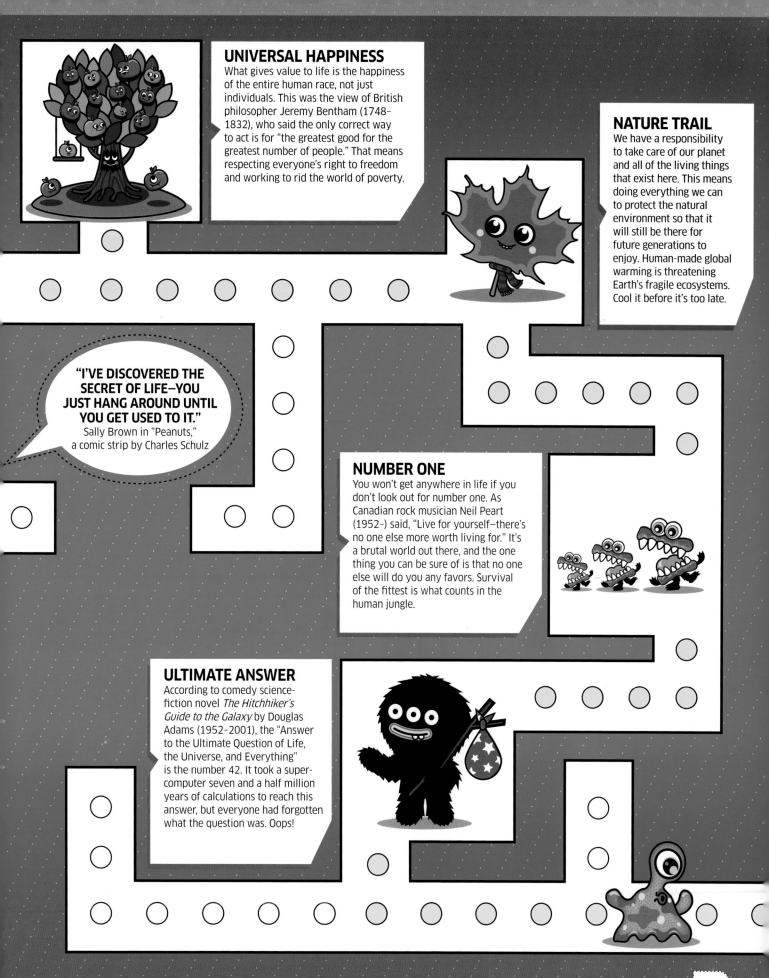

UNIVERSAL HAPPINESS

What gives value to life is the happiness of the entire human race, not just individuals. This was the view of British philosopher Jeremy Bentham (1748–1832), who said the only correct way to act is for "the greatest good for the greatest number of people." That means respecting everyone's right to freedom and working to rid the world of poverty.

NATURE TRAIL

We have a responsibility to take care of our planet and all of the living things that exist here. This means doing everything we can to protect the natural environment so that it will still be there for future generations to enjoy. Human-made global warming is threatening Earth's fragile ecosystems. Cool it before it's too late.

"I'VE DISCOVERED THE SECRET OF LIFE—YOU JUST HANG AROUND UNTIL YOU GET USED TO IT."
Sally Brown in "Peanuts," a comic strip by Charles Schulz

NUMBER ONE

You won't get anywhere in life if you don't look out for number one. As Canadian rock musician Neil Peart (1952–) said, "Live for yourself—there's no one else more worth living for." It's a brutal world out there, and the one thing you can be sure of is that no one else will do you any favors. Survival of the fittest is what counts in the human jungle.

ULTIMATE ANSWER

According to comedy science-fiction novel *The Hitchhiker's Guide to the Galaxy* by Douglas Adams (1952–2001), the "Answer to the Ultimate Question of Life, the Universe, and Everything" is the number 42. It took a super-computer seven and a half million years of calculations to reach this answer, but everyone had forgotten what the question was. Oops!

IS THERE
A GOD?

One of the biggest of life's big questions is the debate over the existence of God. The concept of a single supreme being, all seeing, all knowing, and all powerful, is the basis of many different religions for billions of people around the world. Believers, called theists, insist that at least one God exists, while atheists don't see any evidence for a God. Agnostics say there is no way of knowing for sure. No matter what you believe, where do we start? First, we need to define God. Throughout history, people have believed in hundreds of gods, each with their own roles and responsibilities. The Greek god Zeus, for example,

was the father of all other gods and the ruler of the sky and thunder, while the Viking god Odin was the king of gods and war. All these gods were absolutely real to their worshipers, but today, no one really believes in them. Our question, therefore, relates to a mighty living being with the power to create matter and energy and shape the universe.

HOLY BOOKS
The books of many faiths tell of only one God. God may have several names, including God, Allah, Jehovah, and Heavenly Father, but is ever present and ever perfect.

However, the descriptions of God vary by religion. The Christian God, for example, exists in three parts: Father, Son, and Holy Spirit. The Muslim God, Muhammad, is human in form and the last in a series of prophets who brought God's words to Earth. The Jewish God created the universe but does not have a human form, and God's son, Jesus, is not divine to Jews. The supreme deity in the Hindu faith is a trio of gods, and Hindus worship hundreds more gods and goddesses. So, which God are we talking about? And if we don't even agree who God is, how can it be proved that God exists?

PROVIDING PROOF

Believers say there is plenty of evidence. For example, some people think that the order and incredible complexity of the universe points to a brilliant single creator. Others say there is historical evidence. For example, Muslims believe that the existence of their holy book, the Koran, which is the word of God, is proof that God exists. Many feel that eyewitness accounts of such events as the giving of the

Ten Commandments or the miracles of Jesus, as recorded in the Bible, prove that there is a God. Many others have complete faith in God's existence–for them, belief is more important than proof.

ATHEIST ARGUMENTS

There are plenty of arguments against the existence of God. Science has proven that matter cannot be created or destroyed, only converted. For many, that disproves the idea of a creator God. People also wonder how there can be so much pain, suffering, and evil in the world if there is a God. They feel that if God is all loving and all powerful, there would be no place for bad things to happen. Others feel there is so little evidence and so much contradiction between the different religions that the idea of an all-seeing, all-knowing, all-powerful God is beyond belief. Of course, whether or not you believe in God is entirely a personal decision, and you are entitled to believe what you like, as long as you extend that same right to everyone else. Even Blob

WHAT IS A SOUL?

People describe the soul as the "me" inside a human body. All of the things that make people who they are—personality, feelings, ideas, emotions, intelligence, and a sense of self—come from the soul. This is what gives a person being and purpose. While the body will eventually die, many believe that the soul can live on, immortal and indestructible. In philosophy, the belief in a nonphysical soul separate from the physical human body is called dualism. Do you have a little soul inside you? Let's move on to life's dance floor . . .

WELCOME TO SOUL NIGHT

LIFE AND SOUL
Most soul supporters agree that living humans have individual souls. You get one when you are born and give it up when you die—but that's not the sole belief. Others think that the soul inside a person is part of one universal soul. Many believe that animals have souls, and others think inanimate objects, such as rivers, the wind, blades of grass, and the Sun, have a soul, although the human soul is the most complex of all.

> "BE CARELESS IN YOUR DRESS IF YOU MUST, BUT KEEP A TIDY SOUL."
> Mark Twain (1835-1910), American author

SOUL-SEARCHING
Many philosophers have done a lot of soul-searching on this issue. Plato (c. 427-347 BCE), for example, thought there were three souls: a sensible thinking one in your head, a spirited emotional one in your chest, and a hungry thrill-seeking one in your abdomen. He believed they worked together as one to shape a person's actions and behavior. In the traditional religion of the Fiji people, the soul is a mini person, too small to be visible but an exact copy. In some cultures, people think the soul can exist outside the body.

SOULED OUT

Many people are sold on the idea that every new baby comes complete with a soul. In the Christian religion, God creates all of the souls and gives them out to humans. Believing in Jesus is said to "save" your soul and guarantee entry to an eternal life in heaven. Many folktales tell of selling your soul or making a pact with the devil to exchange your soul for something you want badly, such as power, knowledge, or eternal youth.

LOST SOULS

In the early 1900s, an American doctor weighed dying patients and determined that each person lost 0.046 lb (0.021 kg) at the point of death. Was this the soul escaping? Scientists remain skeptical, but if you believe in life after death, you probably believe that your soul survives the body's physical demise and goes on to whatever comes after: heaven or hell, or into a new body. Some believe that after you die, your soul goes to meet God. It is judged by what type of person you were in life; then God decides the final fate of your soul.

SOULLESS SCIENCE

Perhaps humans are soulless. In fact, there is strong scientific evidence against the existence of a soul. All of the stuff that is attributed to the soul is, in reality, a by-product of neural activity within the brain. Studies have found that different areas of the brain "light up" to show activity when a person does a mental task, and we know which regions of the brain control our consciousness. So maybe the soul is just a figment of our imaginations. However, for many people, this is a soul-destroying thought, and they insist that we all have souls and each of us has a soul mate out there.

IS THERE A HEAVEN?

Good heavens! What is this mysterious afterworld that people talk of? The concept of heaven changes depending on religious beliefs, but it is generally described as a place where people live a joyful and peaceful eternal life, without any of the negative stuff they left behind on Earth. Who wouldn't be knocking on heaven's door? But not everyone is allowed entry, and you have to be good to get on this guest list. Oh, you are? In that case, step inside the ultimate residence and slip into something more heavenly.

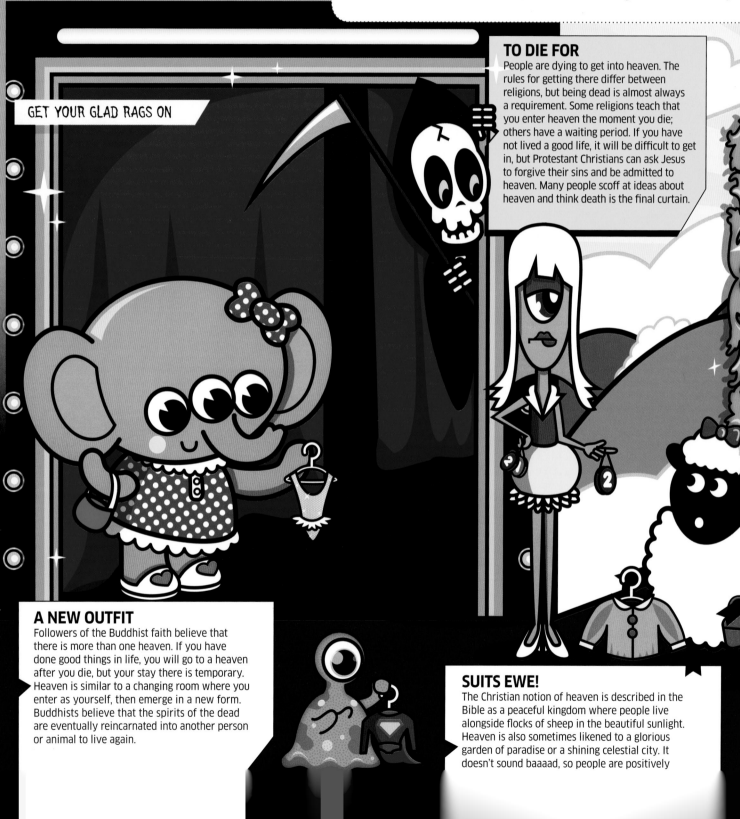

GET YOUR GLAD RAGS ON

TO DIE FOR

People are dying to get into heaven. The rules for getting there differ between religions, but being dead is almost always a requirement. Some religions teach that you enter heaven the moment you die; others have a waiting period. If you have not lived a good life, it will be difficult to get in, but Protestant Christians can ask Jesus to forgive their sins and be admitted to heaven. Many people scoff at ideas about heaven and think death is the final curtain.

A NEW OUTFIT

Followers of the Buddhist faith believe that there is more than one heaven. If you have done good things in life, you will go to a heaven after you die, but your stay there is temporary. Heaven is similar to a changing room where you enter as yourself, then emerge in a new form. Buddhists believe that the spirits of the dead are eventually reincarnated into another person or animal to live again.

SUITS EWE!

The Christian notion of heaven is described in the Bible as a peaceful kingdom where people live alongside flocks of sheep in the beautiful sunlight. Heaven is also sometimes likened to a glorious garden of paradise or a shining celestial city. It doesn't sound baaaad, so people are positively

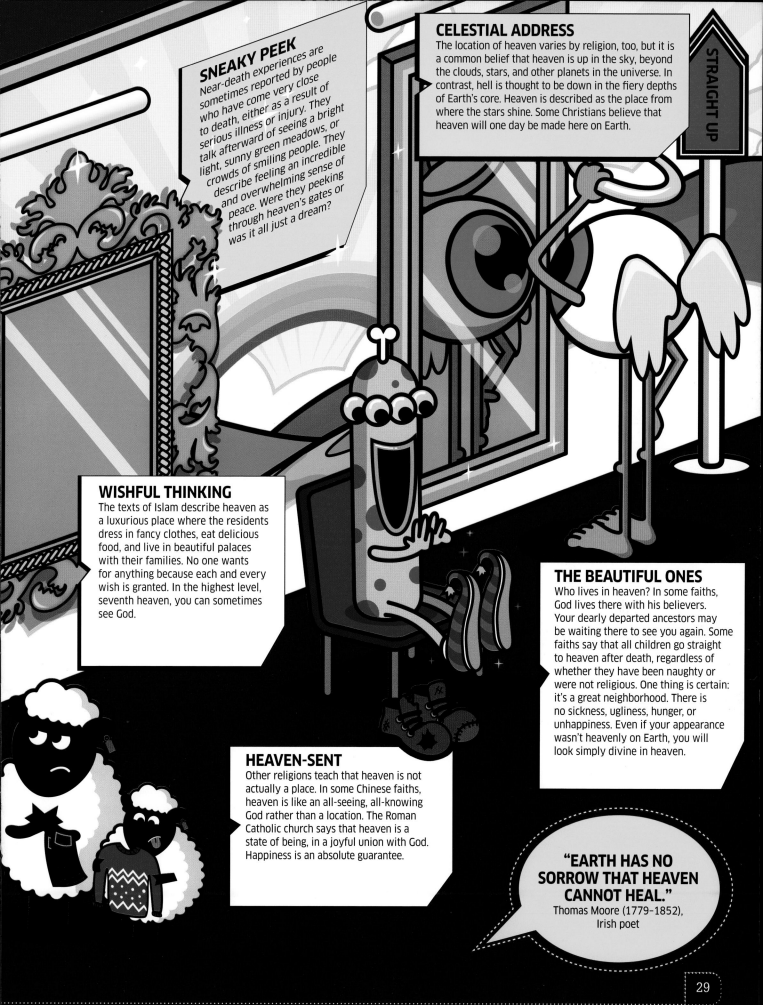

SNEAKY PEEK

Near-death experiences are sometimes reported by people who have come very close to death, either as a result of serious illness or injury. They talk afterward of seeing a bright light, sunny green meadows, or crowds of smiling people. They describe feeling an incredible and overwhelming sense of peace. Were they peeking through heaven's gates or was it all just a dream?

CELESTIAL ADDRESS

The location of heaven varies by religion, too, but it is a common belief that heaven is up in the sky, beyond the clouds, stars, and other planets in the universe. In contrast, hell is thought to be down in the fiery depths of Earth's core. Heaven is described as the place from where the stars shine. Some Christians believe that heaven will one day be made here on Earth.

STRAIGHT UP

WISHFUL THINKING

The texts of Islam describe heaven as a luxurious place where the residents dress in fancy clothes, eat delicious food, and live in beautiful palaces with their families. No one wants for anything because each and every wish is granted. In the highest level, seventh heaven, you can sometimes see God.

THE BEAUTIFUL ONES

Who lives in heaven? In some faiths, God lives there with his believers. Your dearly departed ancestors may be waiting there to see you again. Some faiths say that all children go straight to heaven after death, regardless of whether they have been naughty or were not religious. One thing is certain: it's a great neighborhood. There is no sickness, ugliness, hunger, or unhappiness. Even if your appearance wasn't heavenly on Earth, you will look simply divine in heaven.

HEAVEN-SENT

Other religions teach that heaven is not actually a place. In some Chinese faiths, heaven is like an all-seeing, all-knowing God rather than a location. The Roman Catholic church says that heaven is a state of being, in a joyful union with God. Happiness is an absolute guarantee.

> **"EARTH HAS NO SORROW THAT HEAVEN CANNOT HEAL."**
> Thomas Moore (1779–1852), Irish poet

ARE WE
ALONE IN THE UNIVERSE?

Earth is the one place in the universe where life exists for sure. Yet there are other planets and galaxies beyond our own, so who is to say there is no chance of life elsewhere? Many scientists believe that other life exists, although no definite proof has been presented. Life from anywhere other than our planet is called extraterrestrial (ET). In 1961, an American astrophysicist named Frank Drake came up with an equation, called the Drake equation, to estimate the number of ET civilizations in our galaxy that could contact us. It is estimated that there are about 10,000 potentially communicative ET civilizations. Toward the end of the 1900s, scientists began looking for ET life, from nearby Mars to remote planets orbiting distant stars.

ALIEN SPACECRAFT
Since World War II, there have been a huge number of reported sightings of unidentified flying objects (UFOs), especially over the southwest U.S. and Mexico. In 1947, American pilot Kevin Arnold described flying-saucer shapes in the sky, and afterward, the number of reported UFO sightings escalated dramatically. In the same year, a town called Roswell in New Mexico became a hotbed of UFO speculation after it was claimed that an alien spacecraft had crashed there. Rancher William Brazel heard an explosion on July 2 and went to investigate. He found strange metal debris covering almost 1 mile (1.6 km). The local newspaper published Brazel's claim, but insisted that it was the remains of a crashed weather balloon. Eyewitnesses kept coming forward to tell a similar story, saying they had seen a UFO in the sky and metal wreckage on the ground.

MISTAKEN OBSERVATION
Scientific studies have found that most UFO sightings are genuine observations of objects in the sky, but further investigation reveals them to be aircraft, balloons, clouds, distant planets, or optical illusions. A few are even set up deliberately by photographers looking for fame. It is estimated that between five and 20 percent of sightings are truly unidentified, and it is these that UFO enthusiasts cite as evidence that we may not be alone in the universe.

SEARCH PARTY
An organized group called Search for Extraterrestrial Intelligence (SETI) has been set up to look for proof of life elsewhere. SETI scientists use radio telescopes positioned on Earth to pick up possible signals from ET life. No messages have been picked up to date. About 100 years ago, life was thought to exist on Mars because markings on the planet's surface were interpreted as canals built by a civilization. In more recent times, evidence has suggested that water once flowed on Mars and that the planet might have been suited to life. However, no proof of past organic life has been found, so the search for ET life continues.

HAVE ALIENS VISITED EARTH?

It may sound alien to you, but every year, hundreds of people around the world claim to have been visited and even abducted by aliens. Known as "grays," these unusual guests are often described as small humanoids with big heads, prominent eyes, and gray skin. There is no other evidence that aliens have ever dropped by our planet, yet these accounts continue to mount. If these stories are to be believed, you could be next to receive a strange visitor . . .

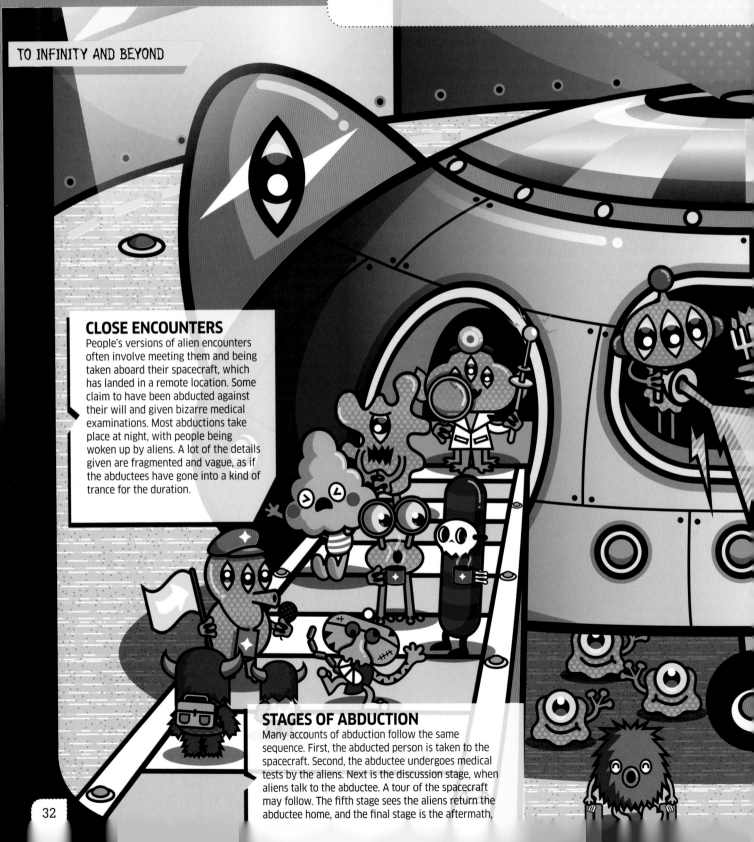

TO INFINITY AND BEYOND

CLOSE ENCOUNTERS

People's versions of alien encounters often involve meeting them and being taken aboard their spacecraft, which has landed in a remote location. Some claim to have been abducted against their will and given bizarre medical examinations. Most abductions take place at night, with people being woken up by aliens. A lot of the details given are fragmented and vague, as if the abductees have gone into a kind of trance for the duration.

STAGES OF ABDUCTION

Many accounts of abduction follow the same sequence. First, the abducted person is taken to the spacecraft. Second, the abductee undergoes medical tests by the aliens. Next is the discussion stage, when aliens talk to the abductee. A tour of the spacecraft may follow. The fifth stage sees the aliens return the abductee home, and the final stage is the aftermath,

SKEPTICAL SCIENCE

If all this seems a bit far-fetched to you, you are not alone. Most scientists disregard these accounts because there is no concrete proof of aliens visiting Earth, let alone abducting someone. They say that these versions of events are the confused recollections of people going through emotional trauma or remembering a dream as reality. Many people are just as skeptical as scientists on this subject.

HEAD FOR THE HILLS

One case of alien abduction has stood the test of time. On September 19, 1961, Americans Barney and Betty Hill saw a spacecraft while driving home to Portsmouth, New Hampshire. Their car began to vibrate, and the Hills felt a strange tingling sensation. Their memories afterward were fragmented, and Betty suffered nightmares. Under hypnosis, the couple described the abduction in minute detail. Their story proved popular and was turned into a book and a movie.

MYSTERIOUS MEN

It is quite common for those who give personal accounts of alien abduction to also claim to have experienced a visit shortly after by some shady suited characters known as "Men in Black." These men insist that witnesses do not share their experiences with anyone. Some say these are government agents who have secret information about alien activity and whose job it is to keep it from the public. A small number of people claim that Men in Black are aliens, too!

WHAT
IS REALITY?

Get real! The answer to this question seems obvious. Things that exist—that is, have physical shape or being—are real, while anything that is made up or imaginary is not real. But it is not quite as simple as that. Philosophers have argued for centuries over the nature of reality. That is because the question they are most concerned with asking—and trying to answer—is how do we know what is real; in other words, how do we distinguish between what is real and what is not? Let's go for a reality check . . .

AM I
REAL?

Pinch yourself—you felt that, didn't you? You know you are real because you have sensory perception—sight, hearing, touch, smell, and taste. You walk, talk, and move around. More importantly, you are aware that you have a mind and being of your own. A great French philosopher, René Descartes (1596–1650), stated that because he had a brain, he could be sure of his own existence. He summed this up in the statement, "I think, therefore I am."

SO, ARE
OTHER PEOPLE REAL?

Other people walk, talk, and move around, like you do. So do robots, but the difference is that robots cannot think for themselves and their batteries run down. Though they are real things, they are not real like us. However, you can tell from the way other people behave that they have brains, think for themselves, and are as real as you are.

WHAT
ABOUT OBJECTS?

You can't walk through an object, can you? Try it with a tree so that you can be sure it has physical reality and is not a phantom tree. However, we know that some things exist, despite the fact that we cannot see or touch them. For example, we deduce that magnetism and electricity exist because we are able to perceive their physical effects on other things. They are real because we recognize their impact.

HOW
ABOUT COLORS?

Color is a visual property of light. It is true that people perceive colors differently—a flower that seems pink to one person may seem orange to someone else. Yet our interpretation of shades of color does not detract from their existence. Similarly, people who are colorblind may confuse certain colors, but that is because they are unable to detect color as most of us do. It does not mean that colors are not real.

COULD
NUMBERS BE DESCRIBED AS REAL?

Some people would say that numbers (numerals) are made-up concepts, and clearly it is true that we cannot see or eat numbers. But if they are just ideas in our minds, how come we can all agree what the number six is, for example? According to Plato (c. 427-347 BCE) and other Greek philosophers, numbers exist in a realm beyond space and time. That's a difficult concept to calculate.

SURELY
VIRTUAL REALITY IS REAL?

No. Virtual reality (VR) is a name given to computer-simulated environments that you experience through the senses—usually sight and sound but sometimes touch, too. They only imitate reality. The goal of the producers of VR software is to make their stuff so convincing that you are ready to believe that it is real.

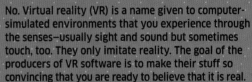

> "REALITY IS THAT WHICH, WHEN YOU STOP BELIEVING IN IT, DOESN'T GO AWAY."
> Philip K. Dick (1928-1982), science-fiction author

WHAT IS IMAGINATION?

Part of the way we think is to form images or ideas in our minds of things and situations that are not physically present or happening, based on knowledge that we have stored in our memory. Some people are better than others at creative imagination—that is, changing or manipulating their mental images to create new ideas. Give it a try . . . Imagination has no limits.

BRAIN BOX

It takes imagination to solve problems and puzzles. First, you mull over what has to be done, scroll through the various solutions in your head, discard the ideas that will not work, test a few of the ones that might, then—hey presto!— you've invented the wheel. Just imagine the possibilities . . .

TASTE TEST

Imagine yourself sinking your teeth into your favorite cake or munching on some salty fries. The mental taste is so strong and enticing that your mouth begins to water in anticipation. We use our "sense memories" to summon up smells, too, so don't think of anything that smells disgusting!

TELLING STORIES

When we remember the past or dream about the future, we're telling ourselves stories inside our heads. Creative writers turn these stories into works of fiction, using their vivid powers of imagination to conjure up interesting characters, exciting plots, and colorful twists.

BIG IMAGINATION

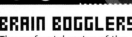

BRAIN BOGGLERS

The prefrontal cortex of the brain is the key to our imagination. Located at the very front of the brain, just behind the forehead, the prefrontal cortex is fed information from other parts of the brain. It is where we make plans and decisions, arrange and organize our thoughts, and have our smartest ideas.

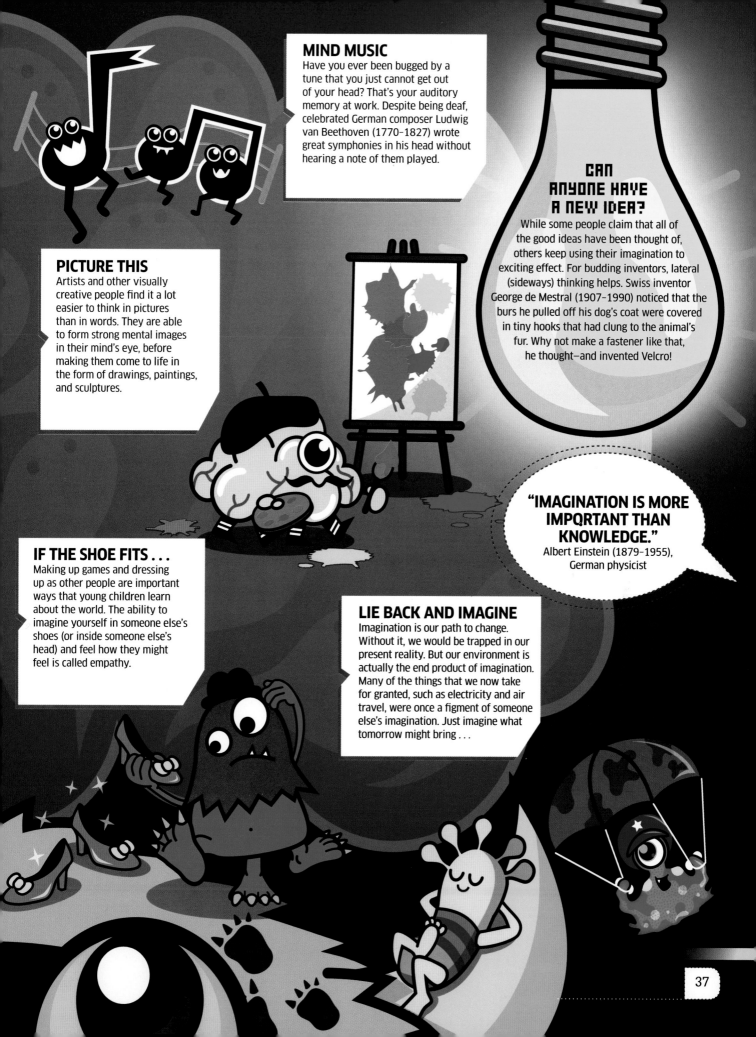

MIND MUSIC

Have you ever been bugged by a tune that you just cannot get out of your head? That's your auditory memory at work. Despite being deaf, celebrated German composer Ludwig van Beethoven (1770-1827) wrote great symphonies in his head without hearing a note of them played.

CAN ANYONE HAVE A NEW IDEA?

While some people claim that all of the good ideas have been thought of, others keep using their imagination to exciting effect. For budding inventors, lateral (sideways) thinking helps. Swiss inventor George de Mestral (1907-1990) noticed that the burs he pulled off his dog's coat were covered in tiny hooks that had clung to the animal's fur. Why not make a fastener like that, he thought—and invented Velcro!

PICTURE THIS

Artists and other visually creative people find it a lot easier to think in pictures than in words. They are able to form strong mental images in their mind's eye, before making them come to life in the form of drawings, paintings, and sculptures.

"IMAGINATION IS MORE IMPORTANT THAN KNOWLEDGE."
Albert Einstein (1879-1955), German physicist

IF THE SHOE FITS . . .

Making up games and dressing up as other people are important ways that young children learn about the world. The ability to imagine yourself in someone else's shoes (or inside someone else's head) and feel how they might feel is called empathy.

LIE BACK AND IMAGINE

Imagination is our path to change. Without it, we would be trapped in our present reality. But our environment is actually the end product of imagination. Many of the things that we now take for granted, such as electricity and air travel, were once a figment of someone else's imagination. Just imagine what tomorrow might bring . . .

WHAT
IS INSANITY?

Insanity literally means "sickness of mind." Another word for insanity is madness. An insane person behaves in ways that other people consider abnormal, irrational, or crazy. It is an all-encompassing label that includes extreme forms of mental illness, such as paranoia (imagining people are following you or wanting to harm you) or schizophrenia (hearing aggressive voices inside your head), as well as eccentric but relatively harmless types of behavior.

PAST TREATMENT

In the past, those people considered insane were locked up in asylums. They were called lunatics (from *luna*, the Latin for "moon") because their symptoms were thought to worsen during a full moon. In 18th-century Europe, fashionable people would visit lunatic asylums and laugh at the antics of the inmates, who were regarded as similar to wild creatures. Insanity is no longer an accepted medical diagnosis. Instead, doctors today recognize and treat a wide range of mental disorders. These include mild anxiety and mood disorders, such as panic attacks, phobias, eating disorders, depression, and mood swings, as well as more serious mental illnesses.

ALL PSYCHED UP

Any word that has *psych* at the front means that it has to do with the mind. A psychiatrist is a doctor who treats mental illness, a psychologist is a scientist who studies the human mind, and a psychopath is a person with a severe mental disorder, often with criminal or violent tendencies. Psychopaths are unable to show emotion or relate normally to other people. They lack a sense of wrongdoing, so they take huge risks and do not recognize society's rules and punishments. Experts estimate that between three and five percent of people show psychopathic tendencies. Although psychopaths often easily tell lies and struggle to keep a job, only a tiny proportion go on to become serial killers, despite their stereotyped portrayals in movies and on television. Some mental disordersare conditions for life, with no outright cure, but most can be managed and treated successfully with the use of drugs, counseling, and other therapies. This allows sufferers to lead relatively normal lives.

MADNESS OF GENIUS

Roman philosopher Seneca (c. 4 BCE–64 CE) said, "There is no great genius without some touch of madness." Throughout history, some great minds have walked a fine line between genius and insanity. Examples include Dutch painter Vincent van Gogh (1853–1890), who was plagued by depression and cut off part of his ear, before taking his own life. One of history's great thinkers, Sir Isaac Newton (1643–1727) probably suffered from psychotic tendencies and mood swings. The story of troubled schizophrenic and Nobel Prize-winning economist John Forbes Nash (1928–) was made famous in the movie *A Beautiful Mind*. Though there is some evidence of a link between genius and insanity, no one has proved this beyond all doubt. Historians continue to research the mental conditions of past geniuses by analyzing their works, letters, and other people's testimonies in order to discover whether madness played a role in their achievements.

DO WE HAVE FREE WILL?

Free will means being free to make choices for ourselves without something or someone restricting us. Most of us assume that we have it, but many philosophers believe that we don't have free will. Instead, they think that our actions are influenced or determined by forces beyond our control. If this is the case, who or what is in charge? Feel free to take a guess.

FREE TO FOLLOW

"WE ARE NOT FREE TO ACT OUTSIDE THE LAWS OF NATURE. EVERYTHING IS PREDICTABLE."

DETERMINISM
Some philosophers argue that, like everything in the universe, every human action is determined by previous events going back in an unbroken chain to the beginning of time. As they believe that all events have been predetermined, determinism is considered to be incompatible with the notion of free will.

FREEDOM TO ACT
A separate philosophical argument accepts that people are bound by the laws of nature but instead stresses that these laws do not compel them to make particular choices. It is up to personal choice as to whether or not to eat a pumpkin, for example. No one is forcing you to do it.

"I AM RESPONSIBLE FOR MY OWN ACTIONS. THE CHOICE IS MINE TO MAKE."

BIOLOGICAL BELIEF

Many scientists believe that we do not have free will. Our genes (nature) and life experiences (nurture) combine to construct our brains and nerve paths. These mold people's personalities and determine how they behave.

"NATURE AND NURTURE DETERMINE OUR BEHAVIOR. FREE WILL DOESN'T COME INTO IT."

RELIGIOUS VIEWS

Many people around the world follow a religious faith and believe that God, who is all powerful, created the universe. In Christianity, for example, the Bible says that God gave the first man and woman, Adam and Eve, the knowledge of good and evil and the ability to choose between them—free will.

"GOD CONTROLS THE UNIVERSE BUT GIVES PEOPLE THE FREEDOM TO MAKE UP THEIR OWN MINDS."

ASTROLOGY

Those who follow astrology believe in fate. People may think they are free agents, able to make their own choices, but in reality, their actions were already decided by the exact positions of the stars and planets on the day they were born. Nothing can change the outcome of this arrangement.

"OUR FUTURE IS ALREADY DECIDED. OUR DESTINY IS WRITTEN IN THE SKIES. SEE FOR YOURSELF . . ."

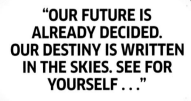

WHAT IS EQUALITY?

The dream of everyone being equal sounds simple enough. After all, everyone is part of the human race, so we should all be the same. The reality is more complicated. When you start to decide what people should be equal to or whether it is ever fair to be unequal, things get tricky. From the outset, babies are not born equal, as their country of birth, home environment, family, and whether they are born male or female all play a role in how their lives turn out.

IN THE BALANCE

HUMAN RIGHTS

A state of equality is difficult to achieve because everyone has different characteristics and is exposed to different situations. Most philosophers would argue that people should have equal human rights to everyone else. The countries that form the United Nations (UN) have decided that all member nations should be equal and agree on a list of rights and freedoms. These include the rights to life and liberty, freedom of movement, and freedom of thought. There is no universal agreement about human rights, however, and some cultures, religions, and countries have different views on equality.

BROKEN LAWS

There are some situations when it is not possible to treat people equally. One example is criminals who have broken the rules of the country they live in. Extreme lawbreakers, such as murderers, are taken away and put in prison, losing their right to liberty. The way they live is no longer equal to someone who has not broken the law. However, as punishments differ according to the crime, they may also be treated differently to someone who has stolen rather than murdered. A thief may get a shorter prison sentence than a murderer, who might be jailed for life and kept in solitary confinement.

EQUAL RULE

Different countries have different systems of government that decide when people should be treated equally or differently. In democratic countries, the government is voted for by the people that live there. The largest party or group of parties that can work together forms the government. For some nations, the ruler is born into a royal family as the heir to the throne. In a few countries, leaders are decided by a group of individuals selected by the predecessor. This happens in the Vatican, where the pope, who is the head of the Catholic Church, is also the head of state. The governments of countries in the UN are regulated to check that all of the people are treated fairly and get the same health care and education, for example.

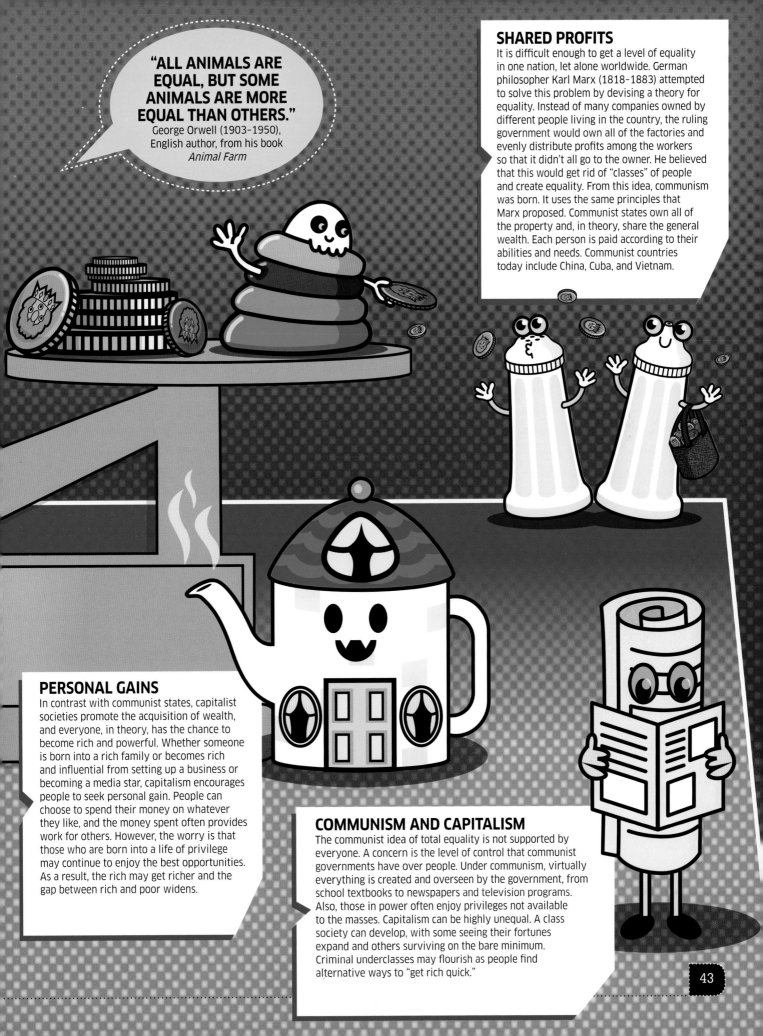

"ALL ANIMALS ARE EQUAL, BUT SOME ANIMALS ARE MORE EQUAL THAN OTHERS."
George Orwell (1903–1950), English author, from his book *Animal Farm*

SHARED PROFITS

It is difficult enough to get a level of equality in one nation, let alone worldwide. German philosopher Karl Marx (1818–1883) attempted to solve this problem by devising a theory for equality. Instead of many companies owned by different people living in the country, the ruling government would own all of the factories and evenly distribute profits among the workers so that it didn't all go to the owner. He believed that this would get rid of "classes" of people and create equality. From this idea, communism was born. It uses the same principles that Marx proposed. Communist states own all of the property and, in theory, share the general wealth. Each person is paid according to their abilities and needs. Communist countries today include China, Cuba, and Vietnam.

PERSONAL GAINS

In contrast with communist states, capitalist societies promote the acquisition of wealth, and everyone, in theory, has the chance to become rich and powerful. Whether someone is born into a rich family or becomes rich and influential from setting up a business or becoming a media star, capitalism encourages people to seek personal gain. People can choose to spend their money on whatever they like, and the money spent often provides work for others. However, the worry is that those who are born into a life of privilege may continue to enjoy the best opportunities. As a result, the rich may get richer and the gap between rich and poor widens.

COMMUNISM AND CAPITALISM

The communist idea of total equality is not supported by everyone. A concern is the level of control that communist governments have over people. Under communism, virtually everything is created and overseen by the government, from school textbooks to newspapers and television programs. Also, those in power often enjoy privileges not available to the masses. Capitalism can be highly unequal. A class society can develop, with some seeing their fortunes expand and others surviving on the bare minimum. Criminal underclasses may flourish as people find alternative ways to "get rich quick."

WHAT
ARE GOOD AND EVIL?

Smiling faces, kind voices, bright colors, warm feelings, and angels are associated with the concept of good. In contrast, evil is the dark side, linked to hatred, danger, and devils. Good and evil are opposites. Bringing happiness and pleasure, good is positive and valued highly, while evil is negative and harmful. Sometimes good and evil can deceive—if something appears too good to be true, it could be evil in disguise . . .

DO YOU
HAVE TO BE RELIGIOUS TO BELIEVE IN GOOD AND EVIL?

Religious people believe that their faith teaches them to recognize what is good and that anything that denies or goes against those teachings is evil. However, people who do not think of themselves as religious also recognize a distinction between good and evil. An action that results in happiness and benefit to other people is good, while something that produces harm and misery is evil.

WOULD
EVERYONE AGREE ABOUT WHAT IS GOOD AND EVIL?

Some things are universally considered good, such as caring for the sick or helping save lives. Similarly, almost everyone agrees that crimes such as murder and genocide are evil. But while we all find the idea of cannibalism, or human sacrifice, horrific today, people were not so squeamish in the past. Most of us eat meat, though some people believe that it is evil to kill animals. Ideas of good and evil are not necessarily fixed in one society, and they may change over time.

ARE
PEOPLE BORN EVIL?

It is tempting to think that a brutal serial killer or monstrous person, such as German dictator Adolf Hitler (1889-1945), must have been born evil. But can a baby really be evil? We all have the capacity to do harm, just as we all have the capacity to do good. Many psychiatrists hesitate to call anyone evil—the factors that turn some people into murderers or criminals are complex, involving their life experiences as well as the makeup of their brains.

AND DO
ANGELS EXIST?

Angels are invisible spirits but are often depicted in human form with long feathery wings. They are thought to be messengers sent by God to protect humans and prevent them from doing harm. No one can prove they exist, so whether you believe in them or not depends on your point of view. However, in 2005, 79 percent of people who responded to an American Internet poll said that they believed they had a guardian angel. Heavenly!

HOW
ABOUT DEVILS?

These bad boys are demons or supernatural creatures that harm humans and encourage them to do bad things. Devils are found in most cultures and religions. In the Jewish and Christian Bible, the devil is called Satan, which means "enemy." Some people believe that he really exists, but others think that the devil is just a symbol of evil. For many people, devils are simply comedy figures with horns, a tail, and a pitchfork seen at Halloween. Trick or treat, anyone?

WHAT IS THE DIFFERENCE BETWEEN RIGHT AND WRONG?

Take a look at the list below. You've probably committed at least one or two of these "crimes" yourself, some of them more than once. It's more than likely you knew at the time that it was wrong to do so and you also recognize that some of these misdeeds are more serious than others. How did you come to know the difference between right and wrong behavior and why is it so important?

PATH OF RIGHTEOUSNESS

HAVE YOU EVER DONE ANY OF THE FOLLOWING?

- pushed ahead of someone in a line
- cheated on a test
- told a story about a friend that you knew was not true
- got into an argument at school
- kept the money when a salesperson handed you too much change
- lied about why you didn't do your homework

GUILTY CONSCIENCE

You know that voice inside your head that nags you when you've done something wrong? Of course, it's not a real voice—another word for it is your conscience. Ignore your conscience at your peril. It has a nasty habit of catching you unaware, leaving you red-faced and stammering, "Sorry, teacher, I didn't mean to break the window." Naughty, naughty!

PLAYGROUND RULES

You were not born with a conscience—it comes with experience. Babies and toddlers have no moral sense of what is right and wrong, so they have to be taught not to grab one another's toys. At school, you soon learn what type of behavior is acceptable in the playground and what is not. It can be tough if you love rough games, but everyone has to observe the rules.

PRAISE OR BLAME

There are two ways of teaching morality—the difference between right and wrong. You can praise someone when they do something right. This will make them feel so pleased with themselves that they'll want to repeat their good behavior. Alternatively, you can tell them off when they do something wrong and punish them so that they know not to make the same mistake again—or that's the idea.

STICK TO THE LAW

Laws are rules that apply to an entire country or community. They spell out what people can or cannot do within that society and lay down punishments for wrongdoers. One purpose of the law is to settle disputes between neighbors and make it easier for people to live together happily. The earliest set of laws dates back at least 4,000 years to ancient Mesopotamia (modern Iraq).

LAWLESS SOCIETY

Imagine living in a country without any laws—people would be able to do exactly what they liked. Of course, it would mean you could do anything you wanted, but although that might sound like fun, think of the dangers. You would have no protection against robbers or murderers. There would be no traffic laws and no police officers to sort out the resulting chaos. What a mess!

CRIME AND PUNISHMENT

Wrongdoers found guilty of committing a crime in a court of law are sentenced to punishment by the judge, who may send them to prison for a set period of time. Imprisonment helps make things safe for others by taking lawbreakers out of the community. It also acts as a deterrent to stop would-be criminals from breaking the law.

BREAKING THE LAW

Here are some of the crime categories recognized by the law:

- **against a person:** assault, robbery, kidnapping, manslaughter, murder
- **against property:** arson, theft, burglary, vandalism, fraud, deception
- **against the state:** conspiracy, espionage, treason
- **against justice:** perversion of justice, bribery of juries, perjury

"THE TIME IS ALWAYS RIGHT TO DO WHAT IS RIGHT."

Martin Luther King Jr. (1929–1968), American civil-rights leader

DOES WHERE I'M BORN MAKE ME WHO I AM?

How did you get to be the person you are? Genetics might have given you traits such as your blood type and eye color, but what about the ways you act, think, and feel? There is a difference between what we are born knowing and doing and what we learn. For instance, all human beings have a biological need to eat, but what they eat, when they eat, and how they prepare food varies around the world. A person's whole way of life is described as culture.

CHANGING CULTURES

CULTURE VULTURES

The definition of culture depends on who you ask. A biologist will tell you that a culture is a colony of bacteria or other microorganisms. A suave and debonair person would describe culture as literature, art, music, and the performing arts. But anthropologists describe culture as the full range of learned human behavior: knowledge, beliefs, art, law, morals, language, customs, and traditions. Unlike instinctive behavior, culture is not something you are born with. Instead, you learn it from your family and surroundings.

> "CULTURE IS THE WIDENING OF THE MIND AND OF THE SPIRIT."
> Jawaharial Nehru (1889–1964),
> Indian prime minister

SHARED CULTURE

Culture helps people feel togetherness and belonging. It gives people a way to communicate and interact with one another and helps establish order in society. Culture gives a group of people an identity that makes them unique. Culture is a very complex whole that can be broken down into smaller traits. These might be gestures, such as a handshake, or customs, such as wearing a veil, or celebrations, such as a wedding.

CULTURE SHOCK

Imagine if you were dropped into a completely different culture. At first, you might stick to your cultural traits of language or dialect. You might dress in the same clothes and eat the same foods as you did before. But the differences are likely to blur over time. You might see yourself as a member of a subculture within the new culture. You would probably adopt some new traits while keeping some of your old ways of life.

COMMON CULTURE

There are certain things that are common to all people in different cultures. Examples include communicating with a verbal language, using age and gender to classify people, identifying people by their family relationships, raising children in a family group, having a concept of privacy, making jokes and playing games, having rules about good and bad behavior, and so on. While all cultures have basic features in common, they differ in the details.

CORE VALUES

Values are personal—they are your own convictions and beliefs. Your values may be similar to those of other people in your family or culture or they may be completely different. Values are not about what is right or wrong but what is right or wrong to *you*. When you decide if something is good or bad, for example, you make the decision through the filter of your values. Culture influences your values, and many cultures share a common set of core values, but your values are yours alone. And very valuable they are, too.

IN THE MIX

Even your cat is cultured. Many animal species teach their young what they learned in order to help them survive. Your cat, for example, may have picked up mouse-hunting tips from her mother. Researchers have shown that animals can learn skills from one another just like humans. But humans are much more complicated than animals. A mix of your culture, values, and biology made you what you are today.

WHAT
IS LANGUAGE?

Without language, you wouldn't be reading this page. You couldn't talk to friends, write a letter, or understand a sign. Language is essential to communication and therefore essential to life. In basic terms, language is the symbols that we learn and use in order to speak and communicate with one another. The meaning of language is based on the idea that everything we might want to name, label, or express is already represented in an existing word. For example, a large gray mammal with tusks is represented in the word *elephant*, and everyone who understands the English language will know it as this. Over time, different meanings may also become attached to the same word, but there remains an original core meaning that is universally shared.

DEAD LANGUAGES
Language can be spoken and written, or one or the other. Many children learn Latin at school, but this is a "dead" language that can only be written. This is because no one is left who can remember how to speak or pronounce the words. Other languages can only be spoken because the words have no standard written form. These languages can be expressed using the international phonetic alphabet. A language that is neither spoken nor written is sign language. This series of silent facial and hand gestures is used to communicate words to deaf people.

ANIMAL EXPRESSION
Though animals may not have a true written and spoken language like we use, it is impossible to deny that they have a form of language. It is clear that animals use noises and gestures to express themselves. People could not claim to understand what it means when a lion roars or a dog barks, but these noises may have meaning within the same species, whether it is to warn of a threat, express hunger, or simply exercise the voice box. Male whales swim the seas making a pattern of regular and predictable sounds that has been described as singing. Scientists believe that this is to attract mates. However, such sounds have not been learned in the same way that people learn language.

LIMITS OF LANGUAGE
Is there a word for every single thing you could ever want to express? If you have tried to convey something and found it difficult to put into words, you will understand the limits of language. This is more likely to affect attempts to describe the exact way we feel in a given moment rather than obvious objects that are easy to define and explain with conventional language. As Austrian philosopher Ludwig Wittgenstein (1889-1951) once said, "The limits of my language are the limits of my world." While we all learn language and recognize the meaning of each word, whether we attach the same meaning to something as someone else does is another matter. Everyone would agree what is meant by the words *tree* or *pen*, but what about *emotion* or *reason*? You may believe that you understand a word in the same way as others do, but more complex words could mean something completely different to someone else. In this way, miscommunication of language can cause conflicts between people. The study of language, called linguistics, investigates surrounding issues like these to achieve a greater understanding of how people attach meaning and communicate.

POWER OF PERSUASION
Orators are public speakers who use clever choice of language to make powerful and persuasive speeches that bring the audience around to their ways of thinking. Famous political speeches by Winston Churchill, Malcolm X, Franklin D. Roosevelt, and Abraham Lincoln have persuaded many who listened to come over to their points of view. When used in the right way, by the power of speech or the written word, language can carry so much weight that, as a result, people choose to swap political parties, adopt new belief systems, or instigate a fundamental change to their lives. So, where would we be without language? Quite simply, lost for words . . .

HOW

DO YOU KNOW THIS IS A QUESTION?

The answer is at the end of the question. In English, the question mark is the punctuation symbol used in place of a period to let you know you are reading a question. No one knows who invented the question mark. Some speculate that when early Latin scholars had a query while writing out text, they added the word *questio* at the end of each line. Later, this was shortened to "qo" and eventually squished into a "q" over an "o" and finally the familiar squiggle. No matter who or how the question mark was created, no one can question how useful it is, along with all of the other symbols we use every day.

WHAT IS A SYMBOL?

Good question. A symbol is an object, picture, or word that represents something else. Your own name, for example, is a symbol for you. Sometimes, a symbol is something material that represents something less obvious. For example, the eagle is a symbol of the U.S.

WHY DO THEY WORK?

Symbols present information quickly and clearly, acting as visual shorthand for concepts such as "stop" and "go." Imagine you are riding your bicycle, for example, and you pedal up to a sign that says, "Please could you begin braking now, as you are about to cross an intersection with traffic proceeding at high speed in the road parallel to you?" By the time you had read all of that, you would have been flattened by oncoming traffic. A red octagonal "STOP" sign tells you what to do in an instant.

WHERE DID THEY COME FROM?

The earliest symbols were probably painted on the walls of ancient caves. Picture writing evolved as a way to record information without words. The first pictograms represented particular objects. For example, an ox drawing stood for an ox. More complex pictograms evolved to represent word sounds, and strings of pictures could be linked together to make a more complex script. Egyptian hieroglyphs, Sumerian cuneiform, and Chinese script are examples of this type of symbol.

HOW
ABOUT NUMBERS?

Most languages in the Western world use Arabic numerals. As symbols, numbers represent quantity as well as certain qualities. For example, Greek mathematician Pythagoras (c. 569–495 BCE) thought even numbers were feminine and odd numbers were masculine. The number "3" is sacred to many religions (the Christian Holy Trinity and the Hindu Trinity), as is the number "7" (seven chakras in Hindu philosophy, seven branches of the Jewish menorah, seven days a week) and "9" (the nine-story pagoda that symbolizes heaven in China).

WHAT
ABOUT PUNCTUATION?

Punctuation marks were not needed with pictograms, but once more complex language evolved, they became essential. The ancient Greek playwrights used punctuation marks to let the actors reading their lines know when to stop. The Romans also used punctuation for pauses, but the person who pulled punctuation together was Aldus Manutius (1450–1515), the Venetian inventor of italic type, who is credited with standardizing punctuation marks. Full marks to Aldus.

AND
MATH AND COMPUTER SYMBOLS?

Simple tally marks for counting were probably the first to be used. In Egyptian hieroglyphics, the sign for addition resembled a pair of legs going forward, while subtraction was a pair of legs going back. German mathematician Johannes Widmann is credited with inventing the plus and minus signs in 1489. Welshman Robert Recorde invented the equals sign in 1557. On computers, the power button is a combination of the binary symbols for on (a "1") and off (a "0"). Binary symbols have been used since World War II to label buttons and switches. The USB symbol was drawn to resemble the Olympian God Neptune's trident. Some people believe that the @ symbol originated in the 500s, when monks used it as a better way of writing the word *ad* (Latin for "at" or "toward").

WHAT
ABOUT TRAFFIC SIGNS?

Not surprisingly, traffic signs have been designed for maximum impact, with a clear system of colors and shapes that can be understood in an instant. Red means something is prohibited, yellow is for caution, and green is for safety. Triangles are for warnings, while circles show that something is prohibited. It's all very symbolic.

SO, WHO WEARS THE PANTS?

Though the battle of the sexes is often dismissed as a source of lighthearted banter and debate, the fact remains that gender roles are fundamentally important to any society. The way that men and women behave differs naturally, but what is expected of them in a specific culture is what helps organize the society as a whole.

THE GENDER DIVIDE

GENDER SEGREGATION

In many cultures, men have a specific role and women have another. One of the genders is usually dominant and has power over the household. The differences between gender roles can be very extreme or barely noticeable. In more traditional societies, the roles of men and women are clearly defined and easy to observe, while in some Western cultures, roles are blurring and merging, so both genders fill or share a variety of roles.

BIOLOGICAL BELIEFS

The traditional dominance of the male in some cultures may be traced back to the evolution of society. Many academics have established a link between biology and social organization. In ancient times, men would hunt and search for firewood, while women would stay with the children. As the offspring were dependent on their mothers for food, it has been suggested that women could not assert themselves among the men and were pushed down the social ladder.

GIRL POWER

Matriarchal societies are quite rare. When women play a more dominant role, they are usually land and property owners. In some matriarchal communities, such as the Minangkabau in Indonesia, men are involved in politics and religion, while women own the land and are in charge of the household and livestock. The land and name is passed from mother to daughter rather than father to son as in patriarchal societies.

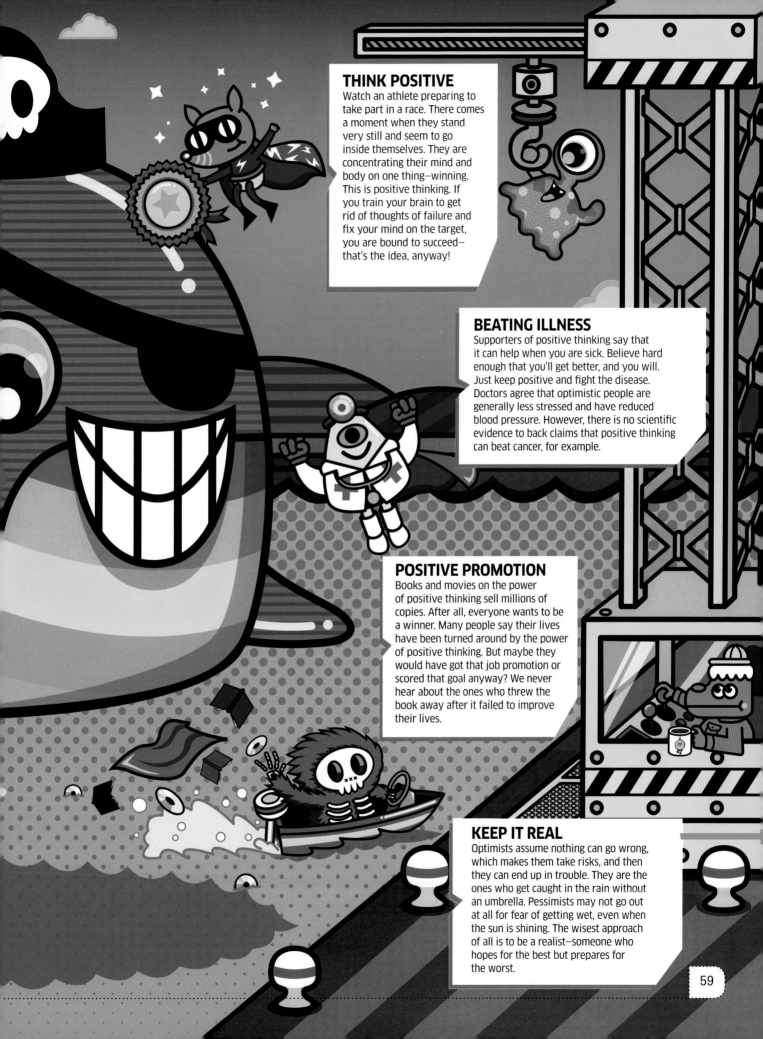

THINK POSITIVE

Watch an athlete preparing to take part in a race. There comes a moment when they stand very still and seem to go inside themselves. They are concentrating their mind and body on one thing—winning. This is positive thinking. If you train your brain to get rid of thoughts of failure and fix your mind on the target, you are bound to succeed—that's the idea, anyway!

BEATING ILLNESS

Supporters of positive thinking say that it can help when you are sick. Believe hard enough that you'll get better, and you will. Just keep positive and fight the disease. Doctors agree that optimistic people are generally less stressed and have reduced blood pressure. However, there is no scientific evidence to back claims that positive thinking can beat cancer, for example.

POSITIVE PROMOTION

Books and movies on the power of positive thinking sell millions of copies. After all, everyone wants to be a winner. Many people say their lives have been turned around by the power of positive thinking. But maybe they would have got that job promotion or scored that goal anyway? We never hear about the ones who threw the book away after it failed to improve their lives.

KEEP IT REAL

Optimists assume nothing can go wrong, which makes them take risks, and then they can end up in trouble. They are the ones who get caught in the rain without an umbrella. Pessimists may not go out at all for fear of getting wet, even when the sun is shining. The wisest approach of all is to be a realist—someone who hopes for the best but prepares for the worst.

WHY AM I THE WAY I AM?

Imagine if everyone was the same—what a boring world it would be. In any given conversation, we'd be able to predict responses, thoughts, and opinions. Thankfully, we all have very different personalities and respond to situations and other people in our own individual way. From hitting it off with one person to clashing with another, we discover that no two personalities match. It is these differences that make life's interactions so rich, varied, and interesting.

ASTROLOGY
In ancient times, the most popular explanation for personality came from astrology and the idea that the time, day, and date of your birth determined your character. Today, many people still follow the readings given for their own zodiac sign and believe that it applies to them specifically. This simplified version can never be very personal, as millions of people share the same sign, but they can't all have the same personality.

NATURE-NURTURE
When asked whether nature (genes) or nurture (experiences) contributed more to personality, Canadian psychologist Donald Hebb (1904–1985) replied, "Which contributes more to the area of a rectangle, its length or its width?" He was making the point that you cannot choose between them. Psychologists agree, accepting that a combination of the two is what makes up an individual's personality.

IDENTICAL TWINS
Genes have a big influence on individual personality, and this has been confirmed in studies of identical twins. As they share genes, any differences between them must come from their experiences (nurture). Results revealed that as well as sharing the main aspects of personality, identical twins share similar intelligence, eyesight, medical problems, and weight. However, genes have less influence on twins' senses of humor.

BIG FIVE

One of the most famous personality tests is called the Big Five, which, as the name suggests, breaks down personality into five main areas. Psychologists use the Big Five to create questionnaires to find out how much of each quality an individual has. They agree that everyone should have at least a little of each.

CONSCIENTIOUSNESS

Reliable and hard-working people usually score high for conscientiousness. They strive to do well, though they can be fussy and sticklers for cleanliness. Those disorganized people who find homework and washing dishes dull and boring (isn't that everyone?) score very low here.

EXTROVERSION

Excitement and fun is what it's all about here. High scores indicate someone who is chatty and confident, with an appetite for danger. Low scores suggest an introvert, who adopts a more cautious approach to life.

NEUROTICISM

This is where the highly strung people are revealed. Those who get worried, excited, or upset very easily are likely to be emotionally sensitive and high scorers here. At the opposite extreme are calm and relaxed types of people, who rarely display their emotions.

AGREEABILITY

Whether you are friend or foe comes to light on this one. Good-natured and easygoing people do well here, while argumentative and bossy types fare worse. As a general rule, people become more agreeable with age.

OPENNESS

New experiences and challenges keep open people happy. They are spontaneous and prefer to try a number of things rather than committing to one. Those who score low here are probably simple types who prefer the familiar and stick to routines.

> "WE CONTINUE TO SHAPE OUR PERSONALITY ALL OUR LIFE."
> Albert Camus (1913–1960), French author

CITRUS TEST

A scientific test can help decide whether you are more introverted (quiet, serious, and reserved) or extroverted (outgoing, adventurous, and talkative). Drop some lemon juice on your tongue and then collect your saliva in a glass. If you made a lot of saliva, you're likely to be more of an introvert, because introverts are more sensitive to stimulation. Take the test with a friend and compare the results.

AMBIVERTS

Everyone's a winner in the personality game. That's because most people are not complete extroverts or introverts. Instead, they're ambiverts, which means that they fall somewhere between the two. You might be quiet and shy with strangers but loud and confident with friends. Also, personality can change over time; for example, it is common for people to overcome shyness as they get older.

61

WHY AM I UNIQUE?

You are different from everyone else on the planet and anyone who has ever lived. But you're not alone—everybody in the world is biologically unique. Though we all look similar, we're completely different from one another in ways that are impossible to tell at a glance. However, new technology allows these unique characteristics to be scanned and recorded. This information confirms individual identities, which proves useful to police forces and security services.

THE ONE AND ONLY WAY

IMMUNE SYSTEM
Unless you are an identical twin, white blood cells in the body's immune system are unique to you. These cells can tell your cells apart from all of the others. That is why when a foreign cell, such as a germ, enters your body, your white blood cells identify it as an invader and go on the attack, engulfing and digesting it.

IRIS
The colored area of your eye is called the iris. Each iris is a unique blend of stripes and gaps. At the age of ten months, the human iris is fully formed and remains the same. Iris-recognition technology scans the iris to produce a unique pattern similar to a bar code, which can be used for individual identification.

FACIAL STRUCTURE
You're not just a pretty face. The arrangement of your facial features is unique to you. Cameras can capture a face in an image, and then an operator figures out coordinates from the features, such as the distance between the corners of the eyes and the hairline pattern. The list of measurements is used to create a unique facial formula to identify people for security reasons.

FINGERPRINTS
Patterns on your fingerprints are unique. They stay the same throughout your life, and if you injure the skin's surface, the same prints grow back. Fingerprints were first used in 14th-century Persia (modern-day Iran), where it was normal to add a print to official documents. Today, in the U.S. alone, the Federal Bureau of Investigation (FBI) holds a copy of more than 50 million people's prints.

BIOMETRICS

The science of measuring and analyzing people's physical characteristics for identification purposes is known as biometrics. Some companies may require a secure authentication process to gain entry. Biometric systems work in the same way. First, an image or recording of a person's specific trait, such as an iris or a fingerprint, is taken. Computer software reads it and turns it into a code or graph. When the person next visits, the system compares the trait with the stored data to determine whether it is the same person.

DNA

Deoxyribonucleic acid (DNA) is found inside body cells and is the material that makes up genes. Comprised of long chains paired in a double helix, DNA works like a code carrying all of the instructions for how the body works. Police use DNA taken from blood, hair, and any other body tissues to discover the identity of people involved with a crime scene.

VOICE

The human voice changes with age and mood, and it is possible to impersonate different accents. Despite this, some vocal tones are unique and cannot be changed. A voiceprint analyzer is used to separate and record these distinctive sounds when a person is speaking. This technology turns the voice into a unique set of patterned lines on a computer.

VEIN STRUCTURE

It's not one for the squeamish, but veins are unique and can be used for identification. Vein-recognition systems scan human hands with a digital camera using near-infrared light. Hemoglobin in the blood absorbs the light, so veins show up clearly as black in the picture. Computer software captures the shapes and positions of the vein structure.

SIGNATURE

Putting pen to paper has very different results depending on the writer. Everyone has their own handwriting style. Graphologists are handwriting experts who believe that it is possible to determine an individual's character by their signature. However, signatures cannot always be used to prove an individual's identity because they can be faked and are often judged only by the eye.

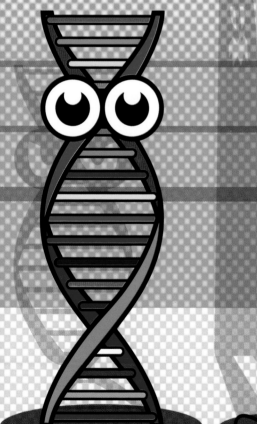

8

7

6

5

4

3

2

HOW
CAN I BE MYSELF?

If you wrack your brain, you might come up with the answer, for it is there that everyone has their sense of inner self. This is the real you, including every thought you ever have. As we use our eyes to look at the world, it may feel like the inner self is located just behind them, but in reality, no one has found a part of the brain that produces the sense of self and all the unique thoughts that go along with it. The idea of self is a brainteaser because although you cannot see it and you do not know its whereabouts, you remain yourself and you cannot escape it.

AM I ABLE
TO THINK AND DO TWO DIFFERENT THINGS AT ONCE?

Of course you can, and there's no room for self-doubt! The brain has a type of long-term memory called procedural memory. This involves skills learned by practice, such as riding a bicycle or playing a game of tennis. The knowledge of how to do these things is implanted in your memory, which means you can pedal and steer or hit a ball without consciously thinking about it. This allows you to perform some tasks as if you are on autopilot, leaving you free to think about other things.

CAN
ANYONE ENTER MY WORLD?

It's a no-go zone. Your views and experiences of the world are completely private. All of your thoughts and sensations contribute to your individuality. No one else can feel exactly the same way as you. Some philosophers believe that while we think we share similar thoughts, we actually regard the world in very different ways. The fact that you cannot enter another person's world means that you will only ever know a filtered version of their thoughts anyway. Close relationships bring a feeling of knowing what someone else is thinking, but neither of you can fully experience each other's worlds.

WHY DO I DAYDREAM?

Although we might think we spend only a short amount of time daydreaming, psychologists estimate that we spend a whopping eight hours a day doing it. Boredom or a lack of concentration are key triggers for entering into a daydream. A lot of the time we don't even realize we have drifted off. Positive daydreams of performing heroic acts can be highly motivating, while negative daydreams of taking revenge can help diffuse anger.

WHY DO I THINK LEFT OR RIGHT?

It might sound mind-boggling, but your brain is split into two very distinct halves. The left half of the brain controls the right half of your body, while the right half of the brain controls the left half of your body. In most people, the left half of the brain is dominant for logic and language and best at hearing the rhythm of music. Contrastingly, the right half of the brain is better at recognizing objects, spatial awareness, understanding jokes, and appreciating musical melody. The left brain controls the right hand, and as most people are right-handed, this indicates that the left brain is usually dominant. However, there is no evidence that left-handed people use their right brain more, and many of them do well using logic and language. Some experts claim that every individual has two inner selves, with a separate self in each half of the brain. Sounds like a split personality!

> "WE ARE WHAT WE THINK. ALL THAT WE ARE ARISES WITH OUR THOUGHTS."
> Buddha (c. 563–479 BCE), founder of Buddhism

WHY DO MEMORIES FADE?

Everyone enjoys a trip down memory lane. Reminiscing about happy moments and special times of life keeps the past alive in our minds. Yet some recollections are so vivid that it feels as if they happened only yesterday, while others are so hazy that any details are difficult to remember. All of our experiences leave an impression on the brain whether we realize it or not, but the strong emotions associated with significant events make these memories easier to recall.

MEMORY LANE

FORGET IT!
An elephant never forgets, but people often do. This shouldn't be viewed as a negative thing, though. Forgetting is as essential as remembering. If your brain didn't filter through the information it receives, your memory would go into overdrive. Minor details would fill your brain, blocking your ability to think clearly. The brain takes control, cherry picking the most interesting and memorable information and getting rid of the rest. That's why the moments that are less meaningful and relevant to us are more difficult to recall.

MEMORY TYPES
There are different types of memory, and these are used at different times. Certain things are not worth remembering, as they were useful only in that second, such as memorizing a train's track number on a departure board. Once you are on the train, this information does not need to be saved in the brain. Other moments are unforgettable. A landmark birthday may stay in your mind throughout the course of your life because it was so special to you.

PROCESSING MEMORIES
The first three years of your life are probably virtually blank on the memory front, but after this time, the brain starts to record memories. It does not have a specific place where information and experiences are stored like a memory bank. Instead, there is a seahorse-shaped area of the brain called the hippocampus that plays an important part in memory. This is where short-term memories first go to be processed, before being turned into long-term memories. No amount of memory jogging can help some people remember the recent or distant past. This condition is called amnesia, and it occurs if the hippocampus suffers damage.

LONG-TERM
This type of memory can last a lifetime. Moments that provoke the strongest emotions, such as great joy or sadness, stick in the brain. Weddings, births, and funerals are among the most common examples of long-term memories. Procedural is another type of long-term memory in which a skill or talent is repeated so many times that it is never forgotten.

REMINDERS AND REFRESHERS

There are many ways to improve memory. One method is to write notes while reading information that you need to retain, and then read the notes again a day later, a week later, a month later, and so on. With repeated refreshers, information is committed to memory. If you still struggle to permanently absorb information, mnemonics is an option. This links potentially mundane information to a meaningful phrase or personal statement, such as Richard Of York Gave Battle In Vain for the rainbow colors—red, orange, yellow, green, blue, indigo, and violet.

> **"MEMORY IS THE DIARY THAT WE ALL CARRY ABOUT WITH US."**
> Oscar Wilde (1854–1900), Irish writer, from his play *The Importance of Being Earnest*

FACTUAL

A form of long-term memory but less personal, factual recollections build up from what you are taught at school. Facts such as the largest ocean or hottest desert may stay with you because you repeatedly studied them for tests. It is important to keep refreshing your memory of factual information; otherwise it will fade over time.

EPISODIC

Remembering certain events, encounters, and experiences is called episodic memory. Your first day of school, a friend's party, or a favorite vacation are all examples. As well as the memory itself, you will recall episodic details, such as the year and location.

SHORT-TERM

This doesn't sound like a useful type of memory, but it's important if you are reading a book, watching a movie, or listening to a friend's story. It may only last seconds or minutes, but that's long enough to ensure your full comprehension.

WHAT IS THE POINT OF SLEEP?

We're always being told that we only live once and to make the most of it. Considering sleep takes up one third of our lives, is it better to forgo it altogether and stay awake so that we can do more? Unfortunately not. Sleep gives the body time to rest and repair while the brain stores the day's experiences. People who are deprived of sleep often suffer from extreme fatigue, headaches, confusion, and even hallucinations. That's why you should stay a sleepyhead!

TIME FOR BED

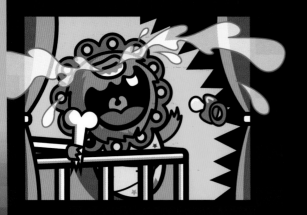

AVERAGE SLEEP

Before the light bulb was invented in the 1800s, adults slept an average of ten hours every night. The amount of sleep required decreases as people age. Young children need about 16 hours per night, schoolchildren need ten, adults need seven, and the elderly need fewer than six. Woken by crying, new parents each lose up to 750 hours of sleep in the first year of their baby's life.

EARLY BIRDS AND NIGHT OWLS

Those people with a short body clock are early birds who spring out of bed first thing in the morning, go to bed early, and fall asleep quickly. However, those people with a long body clock are night owls who love to sleep and stay up late and sleep through their alarm clocks. Inside the brain is the hypothalamus, which signals when it is time for the body to go to sleep.

BODY CLOCK

The amount of sleep required varies from person to person. Everyone has a personal body clock that lets them know how much sleep they need. Some people's body clocks are so precise that they wake up at the same time each day. Research shows that adults sleep anywhere between five and 11 hours a night, with the average being 7.75 hours.

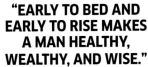

JET LAG

Flying long distances can cause havoc to your body clock. When this clock no longer matches the true time in your arrival destination, you can suffer from feelings of exhaustion and disorientation. This is known as jet lag. One way to get over it is to stay in bright light. As light enters your eyes, it triggers a signal to let your brain know that it is daytime, helping you resist the urge to go straight to sleep.

CREATURE COMFORTS

The animal kingdom has very different sleep patterns, and some are total opposites. While a giraffe needs only two hours sleep a day, a koala manages a whopping 22 hours of sleep. This is because its diet of eucalyptus leaves is nutritionally poor, so sleeping conserves precious energy.

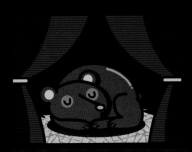

THE BIG SLEEP

Food is scarce and temperatures plummet in the winter, so some animals go into a deep sleep called hibernation. They prepare by eating a lot in the fall, which allows them to live off their body fat, and constructing their winter nest, den, or burrow. Hibernation can last for weeks or months. During this time, the body's temperature lowers and breathing slows down. The animals emerge in the spring notably thinner but strong and ready to find food.

SLEEP DEPRIVATION

A lack of sleep makes people irritable, forgetful, and miserable. One night without sleep can result in a lack of concentration and a shorter attention span. If sleep deprivation continues, the area of the brain that controls language, memory, and planning virtually shuts down. Rats die sooner of sleep deprivation than starvation, and people are probably the same. It certainly can prove fatal—one in five highway accidents is blamed on sleep-deprived drivers.

WHY DO WE DREAM?

You have, on average, a whopping 1,825 dreams every year, though you may not remember them. This is because you have no self-awareness in dreams. The brain's frontal lobes, which produce the sense of self, are mostly shut down. A dream is a series of images, thoughts, or emotions that take the form of a story during sleep. We can find ourselves in any situation in a dream, wondering afterward why we were even there in the first place.

REM SLEEP

There are two main types of sleep. Rapid eye movement (REM) sleep comes and goes during the night and totals about one fifth of sleep time. In REM sleep, your muscles are relaxed, but your brain is highly active and your closed eyes move quickly from side to side. This is when we dream. Electrical activity recorded in the brain during REM sleep has been shown to be similar to that recorded during waking hours.

NON-REM SLEEP

During non-REM sleep, your brain is very quiet, but your body starts moving around. The body uses this time to repair itself after all of its efforts during the day. Every night, we move between periods of REM and non-REM sleep, which helps prepare ourselves for the next day. When we first go to sleep, dreams last about ten minutes, but as we get closer to waking up in the morning, dreams can last up to 45 minutes.

FOLLOW YOUR DREAMS

DREAM THEORIES
Some researchers suggest that dreams serve no real purpose at all, and there is no point in trying to understand why we do dream. Others continue to put forward theories to explain why we dream. Here are some of them:

LONG-TERM MEMORIES
One scientific theory is that dreams are mixed versions of the events and thoughts we have while we are awake. This is the process that ensures the day's memories turn into long-term memories.

DAILY HOUSEKEEPING
Another theory also links the events of the day with what we dream about at night. The idea is that dreaming is a form of housekeeping, clearing away the day's mental clutter so that the mind is ready for the next day. A clear mind allows the brain to absorb new information without overloading.

> ## "DREAMS ARE ILLUSTRATIONS . . . FROM THE BOOK YOUR SOUL IS WRITING ABOUT YOU."
> Marsha Norman (1947–),
> American author

SLEEP PARALYSIS
People affected by sleep paralysis sometimes wake up to find that their bodies will not move. Scientists believe that this occurs because during normal REM sleep, the body is paralyzed to prevent someone from acting out their dreams and injuring themselves. Though the brain has woken up, the body remains frozen in a dream.

NIGHTMARES
We've all woken up, shaken and sweating, from a nightmare. These bad dreams affect children in particular. In the past, people believed that nightmares were evidence of evil magic. Today, scientists blame stress, trauma, emotional problems, or illness. Despite this, some people have regular nightmares unrelated to their waking lives. Studies have found that these people may be more sensitive and emotional.

SLEEPWALKING
Walking while asleep is a mild sleep disorder. Sleep scientists call it a "partial awakening" because the brain is partly awake and partly asleep. Most people do not remember the sleepwalking once they wake up. Some scientists claim that there is a genetic link between instances of sleepwalking in families. A minority of people also eat, bathe, dress, and even drive cars while asleep.

HIDDEN MEANINGS
Some people believe that dreams contain meanings and messages, and if we could interpret and understand them, our lives would make more sense. They could be predicting events or pointing out possibilities for the future, but we have yet to recognize their significance.

PRIVATE PROBLEMS
Other people claim that dreams are a way of revealing the problems that we cannot consciously face. Dreams make people aware of these issues so that they can address them.

OUTSIDE STIMULI
Evidence suggests that the brain registers external stimuli, such as a car alarm, and tries to incorporate this into a dream. Many people have experienced this themselves when, for example, someone is calling their name in a dream and they wake up to find someone trying to wake them.

DO DREAMS HAVE MEANING?

Dreams have been a source of fascination throughout history. Roman leaders believed that they were messages from the gods, while ancient Egyptians felt that the gods revealed themselves in dreams. Today, dreams have been analyzed to such an extent that special dictionaries offer meanings, interpretations, and explanations for thousands of dreams. These are some of the most common dreams—you may already have had some of them.

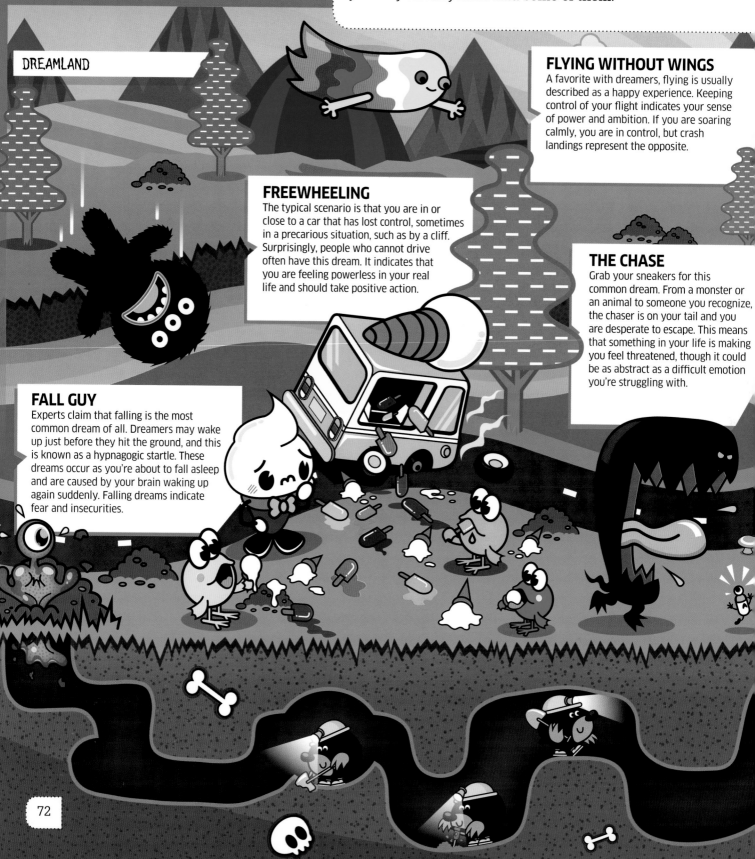

DREAMLAND

FLYING WITHOUT WINGS
A favorite with dreamers, flying is usually described as a happy experience. Keeping control of your flight indicates your sense of power and ambition. If you are soaring calmly, you are in control, but crash landings represent the opposite.

FREEWHEELING
The typical scenario is that you are in or close to a car that has lost control, sometimes in a precarious situation, such as by a cliff. Surprisingly, people who cannot drive often have this dream. It indicates that you are feeling powerless in your real life and should take positive action.

THE CHASE
Grab your sneakers for this common dream. From a monster or an animal to someone you recognize, the chaser is on your tail and you are desperate to escape. This means that something in your life is making you feel threatened, though it could be as abstract as a difficult emotion you're struggling with.

FALL GUY
Experts claim that falling is the most common dream of all. Dreamers may wake up just before they hit the ground, and this is known as a hypnagogic startle. These dreams occur as you're about to fall asleep and are caused by your brain waking up again suddenly. Falling dreams indicate fear and insecurities.

LATE ARRIVAL
You are rushing to catch a bus, train, or airplane, but you don't make it. The dreamer usually misses catching it by just seconds. This is an anxiety dream, and it occurs when you feel you have missed a good opportunity.

SICK LEAVE
Call a doctor! In this disturbing dream, the dreamer or someone known to them is featured sick, injured, or even dying. This dream is most likely to occur when you or someone you know is suffering from an illness. However, if this is not the case, it indicates an emotional time of life.

OVEREXPOSURE
Cover your eyes! Dreams of being completely naked or partially clothed can make the dreamer feel ashamed or liberated. The interpretation of this dream is that you are feeling exposed or vulnerable in real life. Strangely, naked dreams are more commonly experienced by people involved in a wedding.

TEETHING TROUBLE
Open wide and say, "Arrrrgh!" This unpleasant dream affects many people. The dreamer discovers that they have very decayed teeth or no teeth at all. Sometimes teeth are dropping out one by one. This dream is linked to financial worries or the breakdown of a relationship.

DOOMED TO FAIL
No matter how hard you try, you cannot pass a test in this dream. Whether you arrive at the testing room too late to take your test or you take the test knowing you have not studied, failure is the result. This means you are being tested in real life, but you are not ready for it.

GET LOST!
Dense forests, busy cities, or crazy mazes can be the setting for this common nightmare of being lost. Accompanied by feelings of terror, the dreamer searches in vain to find their way. This dream is likely to occur when you have a conflict in your life that you are struggling to resolve.

WHAT CAUSES EMOTIONS?

Life is an emotional roller coaster. In the course of a single day, we can experience moments of happiness, surprise, anger, fear, and sadness. These are instinctive and sometimes fleeting responses to our varying thoughts and experiences. Recalling a special moment from childhood can trigger feelings of joy and nostalgia, while the loss of a loved one can bring overwhelming sadness and despair.

COME ONE! COME ALL!

"LITTLE EMOTIONS ARE THE GREAT CAPTAINS OF OUR LIVES, AND WE OBEY THEM WITHOUT REALIZING IT."
Vincent van Gogh (1853-1890), Dutch painter

PRIMARY EMOTIONS
In the middle of the human brain is the limbic system, which produces our emotions. At its center is the amygdala, a small nut-shaped mass believed to be responsible for our main emotions. Psychologists think that people have six primary emotions. These emotions are so strong that they are difficult for people to mask, so facial expressions reveal a lot about our feelings.

FEAR
Look at this scaredy-cat. He's so afraid of the ringmaster that fear is written all over his face. Fear exposes the whites of the eyes, while blood drains from the face, making it very pale. The mouth may open in horror.

ANGER
Don't get on the wrong side of this ringmaster. Note how red he is—blood is rushing to his head in a typical display of anger. The eyes narrow and muscles pull the eyebrows down and in, causing wrinkles to appear above them. The mouth closes tightly or snarls with fury.

SURPRISE
Random acts or unexpected news can cause surprise. Facial responses may be similar to fear, though there are differences. The mouth drops open and the eyes widen. While fear can be disguised, surprise is difficult to mask, as it is so spontaneous.

TEMPER TANTRUMS
While primary emotions come from the amygdala in the limbic system, other parts of the brain serve to protect us by hiding and controlling our true emotions from other people. These are called the frontal lobes, and they take years to develop, finally reaching full capacity during our 20s. This is why children are more likely to have temper tantrums. Their amygdalas are producing strong primary emotions, but their frontal lobes are not yet ready to prevent them from reacting badly.

JOY
The most obvious expression of joy is a genuine smile. It lifts the cheeks and crinkles the skin around the eyes. Teeth are exposed as the mouth opens. The smile is transmitted to the brain, where joyful feelings become heightened.

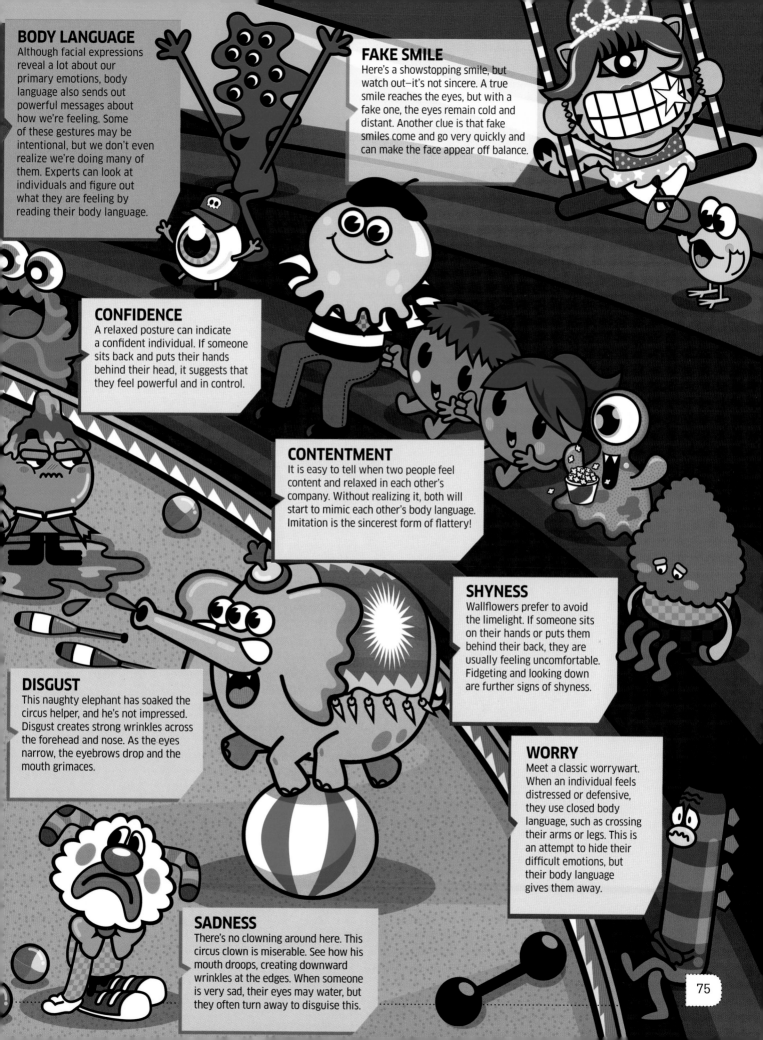

BODY LANGUAGE

Although facial expressions reveal a lot about our primary emotions, body language also sends out powerful messages about how we're feeling. Some of these gestures may be intentional, but we don't even realize we're doing many of them. Experts can look at individuals and figure out what they are feeling by reading their body language.

FAKE SMILE

Here's a showstopping smile, but watch out—it's not sincere. A true smile reaches the eyes, but with a fake one, the eyes remain cold and distant. Another clue is that fake smiles come and go very quickly and can make the face appear off balance.

CONFIDENCE

A relaxed posture can indicate a confident individual. If someone sits back and puts their hands behind their head, it suggests that they feel powerful and in control.

CONTENTMENT

It is easy to tell when two people feel content and relaxed in each other's company. Without realizing it, both will start to mimic each other's body language. Imitation is the sincerest form of flattery!

SHYNESS

Wallflowers prefer to avoid the limelight. If someone sits on their hands or puts them behind their back, they are usually feeling uncomfortable. Fidgeting and looking down are further signs of shyness.

DISGUST

This naughty elephant has soaked the circus helper, and he's not impressed. Disgust creates strong wrinkles across the forehead and nose. As the eyes narrow, the eyebrows drop and the mouth grimaces.

WORRY

Meet a classic worrywart. When an individual feels distressed or defensive, they use closed body language, such as crossing their arms or legs. This is an attempt to hide their difficult emotions, but their body language gives them away.

SADNESS

There's no clowning around here. This circus clown is miserable. See how his mouth droops, creating downward wrinkles at the edges. When someone is very sad, their eyes may water, but they often turn away to disguise this.

Things that go bump in the night, strange shadows on the walls, and someone following you in the dark can all strike terror in your heart. You prepare for the worst . . . As the brain recognizes the threat, your body's survival instincts kick in immediately to protect you. The process is so quick that you are instantly on high alert and ready to face your fears.

WHAT IS FEAR?

NIGHT TERRORS

FEAR FACTOR

Fear has a powerful effect on the body. Under threat, the body's internal processes change rapidly to become stronger and faster. The heart is central to this change. Stimulated by the release of the hormone adrenaline and the quick responses of the nervous system, it beats faster, increasing the levels of oxygen to the muscles and brain so that the body can either confront or escape the threat.

EYES
The pupils widen to let additional light flood in so that the threat can be identified more clearly.

BRAIN
Right away, the brain senses danger and sends nerve messages as a response throughout the body.

MOUTH
As the digestive process slows down, your mouth stops producing saliva and gets very dry.

LUNGS
Breathing deepens and quickens so that the airways inside the lungs widen, allowing oxygen into the bloodstream.

HEART
The heartbeat speeds up so that extra blood is pumped to the muscles and other key parts of the body.

STOMACH
The digestive system goes on hold and blood rushes away from it toward the muscles, creating the sensation of "butterflies" in the stomach.

HANDS
Under threat, increased nerve activity acts on sweat glands to produce more sweat and hands get especially damp.

FIGHT OR FLIGHT?

Like animals, people react to a threat by either fighting it or fleeing it. The fight-or-flight reaction evolved in ancient times, when people would either engage in aggressive combat or run from a large predator. These reactions are basically the same today, though in modern society, the fight reaction is more likely to result in getting angry and arguing, while the flight reaction involves alienating yourself from others.

ADRENALINE RUSH

The adrenal glands sit on top of the body's kidneys, and they secrete the hormone adrenaline. This is always present in the blood in tiny amounts, but when the body is threatened, large amounts of adrenaline are released. The instant adrenaline rush increases the body's heart rate, breathing, and blood flow in response to the threat. In an emergency situation, adrenaline is used by doctors to restart a heart that has stopped or to relieve life-threatening allergic reactions to insect stings.

GENDER REACTIONS

Males and females usually deal with stressful situations and potential threats in different ways. While males are more likely to adopt the fight reaction and react with aggression, females tend to take the flight reaction and leave the situation or find other people to help them. If their offspring are under threat, protective females may turn to aggression.

WHERE DO PHOBIAS COME FROM?

Yikes! About one in ten people suffers from a phobia. Whether the fear takes the form of an object, activity, or situation, it always induces an overwhelming sense of terror. Most phobias are thought to be learned as children—seeing others express a fear of something makes us more likely to become scared of it, too. As identical twins often share phobias, genes may also play a role. Another theory is that phobias develop from a bad experience in early life, which never goes away.

BRONTOPHOBIA
Fear of thunderstorms

VERTIGO
Fear of heights

ICHTHYOPHOBIA
Fear of fish

ROAD TO TERROR

COMMON PHOBIAS

There is a difference between phobias and dislikes of things. A person should experience genuine fear of something in order for it to be classed as an actual phobia. People are most likely to have a phobia involving disease, dangerous situations, or animals. While the first two are understandable, the latter is more complex. Psychologists think that the fear of certain animals stems from our evolutionary past, when deadly or aggressive creatures were a real threat, and people still have the genes that can trigger fear of them. Brace yourself for some of the most common phobias around . . .

ALEKTOROPHOBIA
Fear of birds

OPHIDIOPHOBIA
Fear of snakes

AILUROPHOBIA
Fear of cats

MUSOPHOBIA
Fear of mice and rats

ARACHNOPHOBIA
Fear of spiders

BATRACHOPHOBIA
Fear of amphibians

MYRMECOPHOBIA
Fear of ants

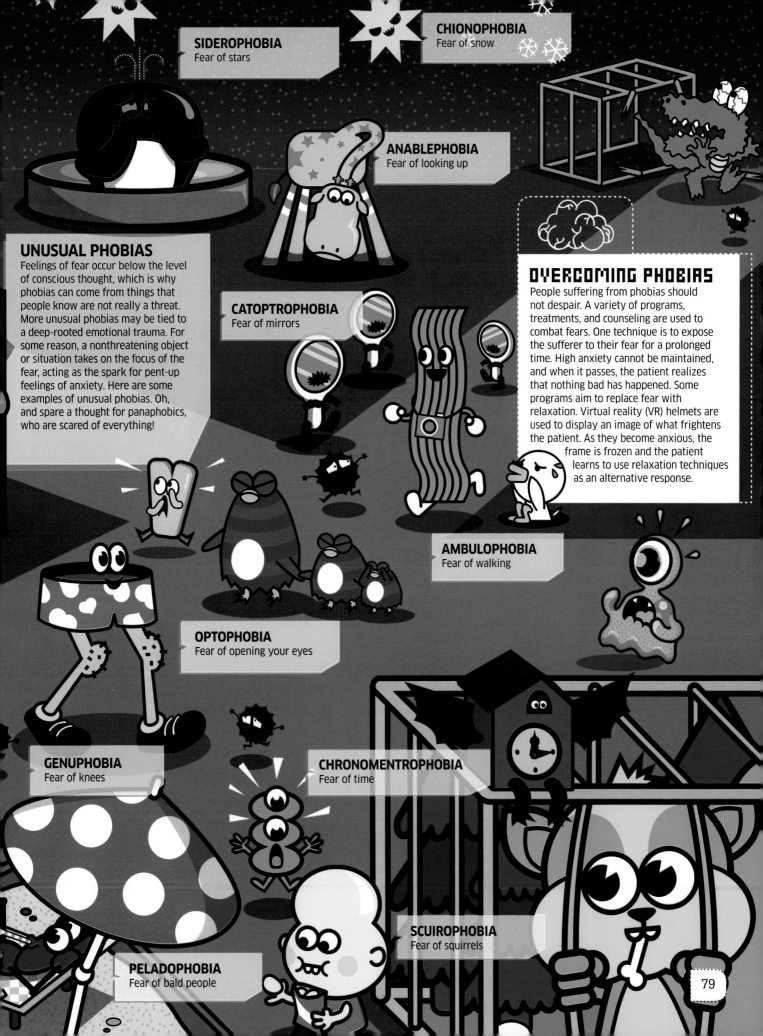

SIDEROPHOBIA
Fear of stars

CHIONOPHOBIA
Fear of snow

ANABLEPHOBIA
Fear of looking up

UNUSUAL PHOBIAS

Feelings of fear occur below the level of conscious thought, which is why phobias can come from things that people know are not really a threat. More unusual phobias may be tied to a deep-rooted emotional trauma. For some reason, a nonthreatening object or situation takes on the focus of the fear, acting as the spark for pent-up feelings of anxiety. Here are some examples of unusual phobias. Oh, and spare a thought for panaphobics, who are scared of everything!

CATOPTROPHOBIA
Fear of mirrors

OVERCOMING PHOBIAS

People suffering from phobias should not despair. A variety of programs, treatments, and counseling are used to combat fears. One technique is to expose the sufferer to their fear for a prolonged time. High anxiety cannot be maintained, and when it passes, the patient realizes that nothing bad has happened. Some programs aim to replace fear with relaxation. Virtual reality (VR) helmets are used to display an image of what frightens the patient. As they become anxious, the frame is frozen and the patient learns to use relaxation techniques as an alternative response.

AMBULOPHOBIA
Fear of walking

OPTOPHOBIA
Fear of opening your eyes

GENUPHOBIA
Fear of knees

CHRONOMENTROPHOBIA
Fear of time

SCUIROPHOBIA
Fear of squirrels

PELADOPHOBIA
Fear of bald people

79

CAN I BELIEVE MY EYES?

We may think we see with our eyes, but we actually see with our brains. When light enters the eye, millions of tiny sensors send nerve signals at high speed along the optic nerve to the brain, which then interprets them to give a three-dimensional (3-D) full-color window on to the world. Most of the time, this works very well, but sometimes the brain is tricked or fooled into seeing something that isn't really there, so watch out!

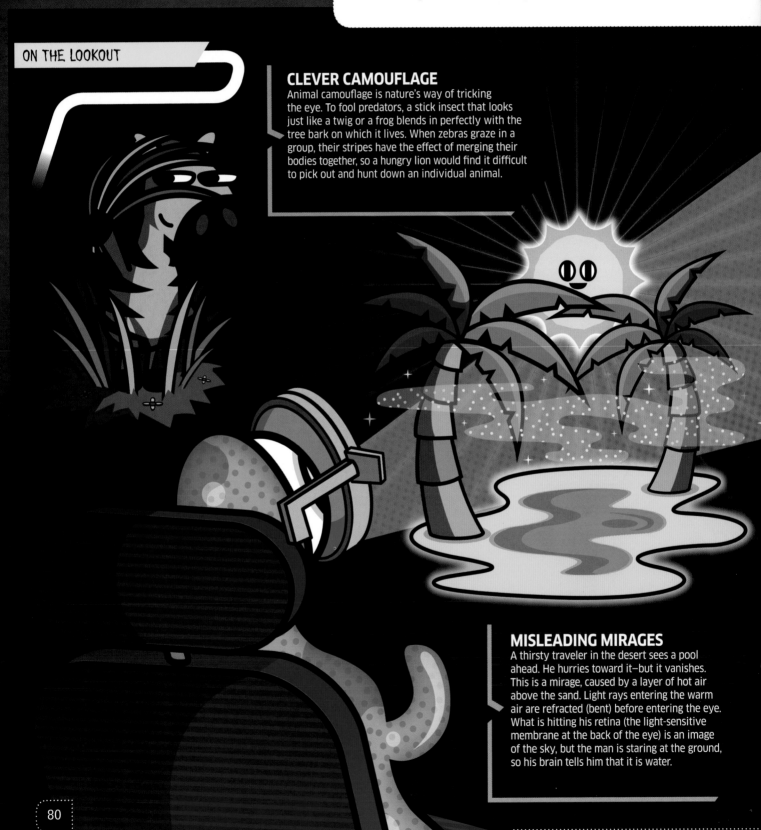

ON THE LOOKOUT

CLEVER CAMOUFLAGE
Animal camouflage is nature's way of tricking the eye. To fool predators, a stick insect that looks just like a twig or a frog blends in perfectly with the tree bark on which it lives. When zebras graze in a group, their stripes have the effect of merging their bodies together, so a hungry lion would find it difficult to pick out and hunt down an individual animal.

MISLEADING MIRAGES
A thirsty traveler in the desert sees a pool ahead. He hurries toward it—but it vanishes. This is a mirage, caused by a layer of hot air above the sand. Light rays entering the warm air are refracted (bent) before entering the eye. What is hitting his retina (the light-sensitive membrane at the back of the eye) is an image of the sky, but the man is staring at the ground, so his brain tells him that it is water.

MOVING PATTERNS

Look at the eye-catching pattern on the right. The circle appears to be rotating, and the rectangles in the circle seem to float sideways. Don't worry, there's nothing wrong with your eyes– it's an optical illusion. The artist has used tricks of perspective (the positioning of the lines and curves in relation to one another) to fool the eyes into sending confusing signals to the brain.

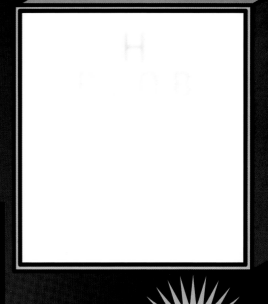

DOUBLE VISION

Your two eyes send slightly different images to the brain, which automatically merges them together–this is how you judge distance. A three-dimensional (3-D) movie is projected in two different colors. When you wear special glasses, the red image enters one eye and the blue enters the other eye. Your brain puts them back together, so they appear 3-D.

FOOLING THE EYE

Artists and architects use a technique known as trompe l'oeil (French for "deceive the eye") to create lifelike 3-D effects. Fruit on a plate may look ready to eat, while a window painted on a wall appears to open up into a garden. The "impossible" triangle on the left seems to be a solid object, but look again . . .

OUT OF SHOT

The camera never lies, or so the saying goes. Yet, from the earliest days of photography, people have played around with images to make things seem other than they are. Russian dictator Joseph Stalin (1879–1953) was notorious for removing his political enemies from the scene by killing them off, before rubbing them out of photographs, too.

DOCTORED IMAGES

It happens more and more in the media today. Digital photographs are adapted in computer programs, such as Photoshop, to make celebrities appear thinner than they are or to put people in a location they shouldn't be. One famous Internet hoax showed a large shark snapping at a helicopter. It was made by combining two separate photographs. The trouble is you don't know what to believe anymore!

PECULIAR PERCEPTIONS

When you wake up and you perceive something or someone that isn't really there, you are probably having a hallucination. These can be momentary impressions of shapes or patterns or vivid sensations that last longer. Often strange and surreal, the experience is usually caused by high fever, a migraine, a food allergy, extreme fatigue, or certain drugs.

SO,

WHAT ABOUT THE OTHER FIVE SENSES?

Sight, sound, smell, taste, and touch are our five main senses that help us experience and appreciate life to the full. However, when one sense is weakened or lost altogether, the body's survival instincts kick in to ensure that the remaining senses become heightened and stronger. German researcher Rudolf Tischner (1879–1961) devised the term *extrasensory perception* to describe any information received from somewhere other than these five recognized senses. Unlike your eyes, ears, nose, mouth, and hands, no clear anatomical part is linked to sixth sense.

HOW

DO I KNOW IF I HAVE PSYCHIC ABILITY?

The extent of an individual's sixth sense is difficult to gauge. Some basic indicators may occur in daily life, such as when the telephone rings and you know who it is before answering or you turn on the radio and know the song that will be playing at that moment. More striking examples of sixth sense include knowing the outcome of a major event before it has happened or knowing when a friend is in danger. Have you experienced any of these things?

WHAT

IS SIXTH SENSE?

Though it is difficult to define sixth sense, psychologists agree that we all have it. The trick is learning to open your mind in order to recognize it. Sixth sense describes our powers of intuition. Any time you have a feeling, hunch, or gut instinct about something for no apparent reason, it is likely to be your sixth sense at work. While skeptics dismiss examples of sixth sense as mere coincidence, psychic experts are certain that these subtle abilities lie within all of us and are just waiting to be developed.

CAN I
IMPROVE MY PSYCHIC ABILITY?

You certainly can, though the best way is to start small. Think about one example of a phenomenon that has happened to you and keep it as your focus. If, on one occasion, you knew the song that was playing before you turned on the radio, relive the moment in your head again and again. Now you can begin testing yourself. Each time you go to turn on the radio, write down the song that will be playing and record the results. Alternatively, with a deck of cards, try to predict which numbers you will turn over and chart your progress.

IS IT
POSSIBLE TO READ OTHER PEOPLE'S THOUGHTS?

Just imagine what would happen if people could read your thoughts! The normal way to communicate is just to speak and listen, but some psychic experts claim that it is possible for people to share thoughts without verbalizing them. Called telepathy, this process relies on using the sixth sense to pass information between two people. To date, tests have been unable to prove for certain the existence of telepathy.

DO
ANIMALS HAVE A SIXTH SENSE?

Animal communicators are special psychics who believe that silent exchanges are possible with pets. They claim that telepathy between owner and pet allows information or pictures to be passed back and forth. However, this is not easy to back up with evidence. Owners traveling home may find their dog sitting by the door waiting for them and interpret this as proof of sixth sense. Others dismiss it as an animal becoming familiar with its owner's routine. The strongest argument for sixth sense is the number of lost cats and dogs that manage to find their way home, sometimes over great distances and even when their owners have changed location. The theory is that many animals have a deep psychic connection with their owners.

DOES
PRACTICE MAKE PERFECT?

An unknown ancient Roman author wrote, "Practice is the best of all instructors." So, is it true that the more you practice something the better you become? Could we all be superstars in our chosen field if we put the effort in and practice as much as possible? If you decided to become an Olympic athlete, a musical genius, a prima ballerina, or a chess whit, could you achieve your dream through practice alone? The expression "practice makes perfect" has been in use for centuries, but is there any reason to believe that it is true? Is doing something over and over again the only way to do it well?

TRAIN YOUR BRAIN
Scientists researching the way that our brains control our bodies have reported that repetition—practice—can help us perfect our moves. Performing a motor skill involves the premotor cortex area of the brain. The brain plans how we are going to move to achieve a goal, and then our limbs follow its instructions and move. If you move in the right way, your brain stores the instructions so that you can do it again correctly. Even if you mess up, it remembers that, too. Practice helps you train your muscles to perform a task in a certain way.

MAGIC NUMBER

It is incredible but true—researchers have figured out the magic number of hours needed to turn someone into an expert. They say you need to practice for 10,000 solid hours, which works out at around three hours a day for ten years. There are countless examples of how putting in 10,000 hours of dedicated hard work will get you to the top of your game, whatever that game may be. However, as sports coaches such as American football legend Vince Lombardi (1913-1970) like to point out, only "perfect" practice makes perfect. If you practice incorrectly, you might make the same mistake over and over again. If you make mistakes every time you practice, you're practicing mistakes as much as the right stuff. It's tough to be consistently perfect, though. Once our brains have decided exactly how we need to move to serve a smash or score a goal, we don't get it right every single time. Scientists think this is because our nervous systems are not made to do the same thing over and over. Instead, we adapt to change. Small differences in the way the brain plans and calculates a movement cause a variation in the actual movement. While a champion athlete may strive to make every move consistent, most of us cannot move in the same way every time.

PUTTING IT INTO PRACTICE

So, if you have 10,000 hours to spare you're going to be a superstar, right? Maybe. But you'll still need natural ability. Being in the right time and the right place helps, too, so you can take advantage of the opportunities that life presents you. Some people think luck plays a role, too. Practice makes perfect sense, though, if you want to get better at something. Good luck!

CAN I BE BRAINWASHED?

You can shampoo your hair or take a bubble bath, but can you be brainwashed? Brainwashing (or mind control) is when someone takes control of another person's thoughts and actions against their will. It may be used to force the victim to abandon a political, social, or religious belief and accept the brainwasher's point of view. Or, do you think this is all hogwash? Put your brain into gear and read on . . .

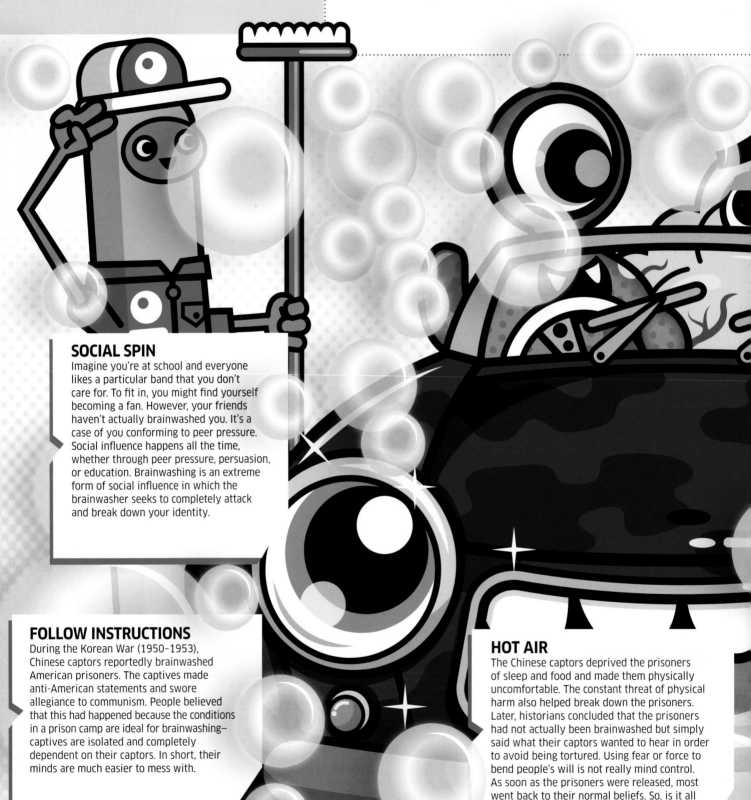

SOCIAL SPIN
Imagine you're at school and everyone likes a particular band that you don't care for. To fit in, you might find yourself becoming a fan. However, your friends haven't actually brainwashed you. It's a case of you conforming to peer pressure. Social influence happens all the time, whether through peer pressure, persuasion, or education. Brainwashing is an extreme form of social influence in which the brainwasher seeks to completely attack and break down your identity.

FOLLOW INSTRUCTIONS
During the Korean War (1950–1953), Chinese captors reportedly brainwashed American prisoners. The captives made anti-American statements and swore allegiance to communism. People believed that this had happened because the conditions in a prison camp are ideal for brainwashing–captives are isolated and completely dependent on their captors. In short, their minds are much easier to mess with.

HOT AIR
The Chinese captors deprived the prisoners of sleep and food and made them physically uncomfortable. The constant threat of physical harm also helped break down the prisoners. Later, historians concluded that the prisoners had not actually been brainwashed but simply said what their captors wanted to hear in order to avoid being tortured. Using fear or force to bend people's will is not really mind control. As soon as the prisoners were released, most went back to their normal beliefs. So, is it all just a bunch of hot air?

FULL CYCLE

A famous suspected victim of brainwashing was American publishing heiress Patty Hearst (1954–). A terrorist group captured her in the 1970s and locked her in a closet. She was kept hungry and tired, tortured, and made completely dependent on her kidnappers. Within two months, she gave up her family, changed her name, and joined the kidnappers in a bank heist. Despite this, Hearst also did a complete turnaround and changed back to her old self after spending two years in prison. Perhaps brainwashing is just a bunch of spin?

DIRTY DEEDS

In movies and books, brainwashing victims are put under hypnosis—a state similar to deep sleep, induced by another person. The hypnotized person is then trained to do something extreme—for example, assassinate someone—when the hypnotist sets off a trigger of some kind. Already, stage hypnotists can manipulate people's behavior to do things that are out of character. In the future, perhaps, an evil neurosurgeon may figure out how to implant something in the brain to control it.

HIGH-PRESSURE WASH

During the 1960s and 1970s, nonmainstream religious groups emerged that were especially appealing to young people who were open to hearing new ideas. Many parents, upset by the drastic changes in their children's beliefs or actions, claimed that these religious "cults" had brainwashed their children. In extreme cases, parents kidnapped their kids and sent them to be "reprogrammed" back to normal. In truth, the religious recruiters had convinced their vulnerable victims to give up control of their thoughts and actions through extreme emotional pressure.

WASHOUT

After the Korean War was over, the American Central Intelligence Agency (CIA) conducted a series of secret mind-control experiments. Among other things, they wanted to figure out if brainwashing was a possible way to obtain information during an interrogation. Reports claim that they studied a range of techniques, from sleep deprivation and isolation to giving mind-altering drugs to the test group of volunteers. Although the tests were interesting in theory, no one knows exactly what happened because the files were most likely destroyed in the 1970s. What a washout.

WHAT
IS BEAUTY?

It sounds like an easy question to answer—a breathtaking sunset, a glimpse of a tiger, a glowing smile, or a bouquet of fresh flowers. But what makes these things beautiful? Shape, size, and color are some of the aspects of beautiful things that give pleasure. Though people usually find beauty in what they see with their eyes, it is also possible to describe a striking piece of music as beautiful. Mathematicians often speak of the beauty of numbers, while poets and writers can find great inspiration in nature's sounds and smells. These differing ideas of beauty are summed up by the expression "Beauty is in the eye of the beholder." This affirms that

everyone has their own idea of what is beautiful. Two people looking at pictures of fashion models may disagree over who is beautiful. In general, we absorb our ideas of beauty from the images we see all around us—in paintings, books and magazines, movies, and television—as well as what we learn from other people about what they find beautiful.

PERSPECTIVE AND TIME
Ideas of beauty (sometimes called aesthetics) change over time. During the 18th century's romantic movement, people found mountains ugly and threatening, but today, they are

"Everything has beauty, but not everyone sees it." Confucius (551–479 BCE)

picture-post card material. As ideas of beauty change, so does the value that society places on it. The paintings by Dutch artist Vincent van Gogh (1853–1890) were once thought crude and shocking. Today, his bright canvases are considered beautiful. They are also among the world's most valuable works of art.

PRETTY AS A PICTURE

Artists have always painted beautiful women, but they rarely match our modern perceptions of beauty. For a start, they are much plumper than is considered attractive today. In the past, if you were overweight, it meant you had a lot to eat and were therefore rich—and desirable. Today, the opposite is true. The thinner you are, the more time you may have spent in expensive gyms working off the weight. Similarly, pale skin was once considered the height of beauty because tanned skin was associated with people who worked outside. This changed when beach vacations became the mark of the wealthy, and suntanned skin was deemed attractive. Girls belonging to the Padaung people of eastern Myanmar

(Burma) were fitted with bronze neck rings from the age of about five. New rings were added at certain times, so when a girl was old enough to marry, her neck had been stretched by 10 in (25 cm). This probably seems ugly and deforming to people from other cultures, but not to the Padaung. Neck rings enhanced a woman's beauty and also gave her family social status.

PERFECT SYMMETRY

Scientific studies show that most people find the evenly balanced features of symmetrical faces more beautiful than asymmetric ones. Biologists believe that there is a genetic reason for this. Disease and infections during physical growth can cause small imperfections, so if someone has smooth and even features, it is a sign that they have a good immune system and will produce healthy babies. The wish to follow a media ideal of "perfect" beauty makes some people resort to plastic surgery to change their facial features or body parts. However, by conforming to stereotypes, a person's natural beauty—what makes them unique and special—is lost.

WHAT IS LOVE?

In her famous poem "How do I love thee? Let me count the ways . . .," English poet Elizabeth Barrett Browning (1806–1861) expresses the wide variety of feelings she has for her partner. The English language uses the word *love* to describe not only this romantic love but all of the other ways there are to love. So, let's count the ways . . .

FOLLOW YOUR HEART

FALLING IN LOVE

When a couple falls in love, they share an intensity of emotions that includes passion (sexual attraction), intimacy (close friendship and the exchange of secrets), and commitment (the shared desire to stay together). According to biologists, they are fulfilling their natural drive to have children and pass on their genes to the next generation. Cue the violins . . .

"ALL YOU NEED IS LOVE."

John Lennon (1940–1980) and Paul McCartney (1942–), British songwriters

ABSTRACT AFFECTION

Another type of love is when people identify their own happiness with an abstract idea or cause, such as their country, freedom, or a favorite charity. The attachment can run very deep—try asking a football fan how he feels when his team loses!

ANIMAL ATTRACTION

Keeping animals as pets can give people a source of love and companionship, especially for those living alone. Doctors say that petting animals releases feel-good hormones and reduces stress levels. If you are lucky enough, swimming with dolphins will produce a similar effect!

SIBLING BOND

The bonds of love and affection between brothers and sisters can be very strong, even after long periods of separation. When siblings who are parted in childhood meet years later as adults in crowded airport settings, they often immediately recognize each other.

HOLY DEVOTION

For people of a religious faith, love is of a supernatural or sacred nature. They show their love for God in regular worship and prayer and in other ways during their daily lives, such as doing volunteer work or caring for people who are sick or in trouble.

FRIENDS FOREVER

As the saying goes, "Make new friends, but keep the old, one is silver, the other is gold." Close friends can be more open with each other than they are with partners or family members. Long-lasting ties of affection mean that they trust each other and feel able to speak honestly without the risk of hurt feelings.

BROKENHEARTED

Being in love with someone who does not feel the same way about you is called unrequited love, and it can be a very painful experience. Unfortunately, most people go through unrequited love, especially during adolescence and early adulthood. Over time, hearts mend, and people go on to love again.

BABY LOVE

Psychologists believe that the close bonds of love forged between child and parent, or other family members, during the early years of life has a lasting influence on their later emotional and social development. Many mothers and fathers describe the love for their newborn child as stronger than any other they have known.

CHEMICAL RUSH

The classic symptoms of falling in love are sweating palms, pounding heart, loss of appetite, lack of concentration, and sleepless nights. This is due to the release of a brain chemical called phenylethylamine (PEA). Also found in food such as chocolate, PEA causes a sudden rush of excitement and stimulates the release of other chemicals—dopamine, norepinephrine, and serotonin. They surge together in the brain to create an emotional "high" that lasts for up to three years.

SMITTEN BY SMELL

People may choose partners who will give their children the best start in life—by smelling them! Everyone's immune system is controlled by a unique set of MHC genes. Research shows that people tend to prefer the body odor of a partner whose MHC genes are very different from their own. It could be because children born to parents with dissimilar immune systems are likely to have strong immune systems to fight illness.

ANCIENT CRAFTS

Creating and decorating a vase or pot was not an artistic process for the ancient Greeks. Their endeavors were for practical reasons, and the objects were always put to good use. It is only in recent times that people have begun to consider these early works as art—ancient peoples never viewed their crafts this way.

RELIGIOUS WORKS

During the 1400s, elaborate books were handcrafted across Europe by hard-working monks. Religious works were rewritten alongside beautiful illustrations. It was a laborious process for the monks, who were called artisans (skilled workers) rather than artists.

ABSTRACT ART

Freedom of expression was prominent by the 1800s. Art reflected the artists' personal view of the world, producing a much broader body of creative work. European traditions were ignored as artists enjoyed new experimentation. Art became abstract, evident in the famous paintings of mixed-up faces by Spain's Pablo Picasso (1881–1973).

TRAINING ACADEMIES

As artists gained approval in wider society, new academies of art were established in Europe. The first was opened in Italy in 1563, and these academies soon spread across the continent. Subjects including human anatomy and geometry were taught to assist artists with their development, though the concept of art remained limited.

ART APPRECIATION

The perception of painters and sculptors as artists came to light during the 1500s. Captive audiences showed appreciation for new creations, and previously anonymous artists received recognition. Leading the way was Italian Michelangelo (1475–1564), who won the hearts of many with his spectacular painting on the ceiling of the grand Sistine Chapel, covering 12,000 sq. ft. (1,100 m²).

OUTDOOR EXHIBITS

Art is not always displayed in a gallery in the 21st century. What was previously dismissed as graffiti may now be called art, with U.K. artist Banksy creating striking and recognizable images on public buildings. His work demonstrates that anything goes in today's art scene.

REDEFINING ART

The traditional view of art as something beautiful was flushed away in 1917 when French artist Marcel Duchamp (1887–1968) signed a porcelain men's toilet with a false name and exhibited it. The controversial piece was true to the 20th-century belief that anything was art if the artist deemed it so. The response of the audience and critics was completely another matter!

> **"A PICTURE IS WORTH A THOUSAND WORDS."**
> Napoleon Bonaparte (1769–1821), emperor of France

WHAT IS ART?

Time has changed the definition of art. In the ancient past, handcrafted objects were not perceived as art, nor was the creator considered an artist. Over the centuries, the notion of the artist has developed, along with a broad range of artistic styles. From paintings and sculptures to photography and architecture, today's art challenges traditional thought. Expression and imagination allow artists to break new—and sometimes controversial—ground.

ARTISTIC INTERPRETATION

With artists becoming ever more creative and expressive, the perceptions of what art is has become very contentious. In defining art, a line must be drawn somewhere, but the decision is up to the individual. The desk you sit at was designed and produced by someone. The clothes you wear were designed and manufactured by another. The book you are reading was designed and written by someone. The list of examples is endless. While some would interpret these things as art, others would dismiss them as functional items, instead claiming that true art must be in a traditional form, such as a painting or sculpture. So, where do you draw the line?

CHANGING VALUES

Art competitions attract a range of weird and wonderful entries. The U.K.'s Turner Prize famously goes against traditional concepts of art, displaying flashing lights, preserved sharks, and unmade beds. However, it is not only the type of art on display that has changed beyond recognition. The value attached to different works has rocketed with time. In 1990, a painting by Dutch artist Vincent van Gogh (1853-1890) sold for about $78 million, though in his lifetime he could not make a living from his work.

HOW DO COLORS MAKE YOU FEEL?

At the most basic level, color brightens up the world, making it a more fascinating and fabulous place. But beyond this, color is involved in virtually every aspect of our lives. It's more than just adding a splash of color to an outfit or choosing a color scheme for a room; color can also convey messages, create sensations, and influence decisions, as well as lifting, changing, or worsening our moods.

OVER THE RAINBOW

MAKING WAVES

Color is how our eyes view light. All light consists of waves of differing lengths, which produce colors. The human eye has 120 million rods and six million cones. Rods perceive images as black, white, and gray. Each cone has a pigment sensitive to red, green, or blue. Short-wavelength cones absorb blue light, middle ones absorb green, and long ones absorb red. All of the other colors we see are between red and blue.

SCREEN SPECTRUM

If the visible area of the light spectrum is divided into thirds, the dominant colors are red, green, and blue. These three are regarded as the primary colors of the visible light spectrum. The colors viewed on television are produced using a system called RGB (red, green, and blue). Despite the glorious technicolor of television, these three colors make up all of the different tones of the programs.

TRUE COLORS

Swiss color psychologist Dr. Maxo Lüscher (1923–) believes that colors can reflect feelings. Red expresses excitement and independence, while yellow indicates optimism and creativity. Green shows persistence and assertiveness, blue conveys peace and sensitivity, and violet evokes mysticism and intuition. At the other end of the spectrum, brown reveals discomfort and black represents rebelliousness.

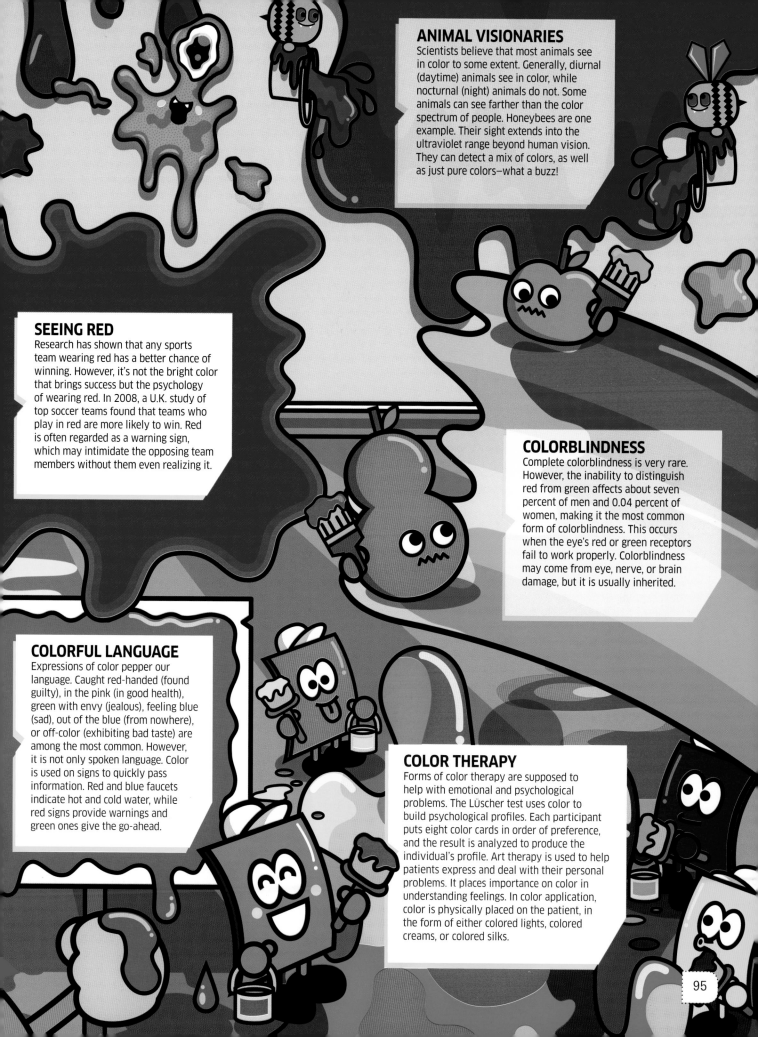

ANIMAL VISIONARIES

Scientists believe that most animals see in color to some extent. Generally, diurnal (daytime) animals see in color, while nocturnal (night) animals do not. Some animals can see farther than the color spectrum of people. Honeybees are one example. Their sight extends into the ultraviolet range beyond human vision. They can detect a mix of colors, as well as just pure colors—what a buzz!

SEEING RED

Research has shown that any sports team wearing red has a better chance of winning. However, it's not the bright color that brings success but the psychology of wearing red. In 2008, a U.K. study of top soccer teams found that teams who play in red are more likely to win. Red is often regarded as a warning sign, which may intimidate the opposing team members without them even realizing it.

COLORBLINDNESS

Complete colorblindness is very rare. However, the inability to distinguish red from green affects about seven percent of men and 0.04 percent of women, making it the most common form of colorblindness. This occurs when the eye's red or green receptors fail to work properly. Colorblindness may come from eye, nerve, or brain damage, but it is usually inherited.

COLORFUL LANGUAGE

Expressions of color pepper our language. Caught red-handed (found guilty), in the pink (in good health), green with envy (jealous), feeling blue (sad), out of the blue (from nowhere), or off-color (exhibiting bad taste) are among the most common. However, it is not only spoken language. Color is used on signs to quickly pass information. Red and blue faucets indicate hot and cold water, while red signs provide warnings and green ones give the go-ahead.

COLOR THERAPY

Forms of color therapy are supposed to help with emotional and psychological problems. The Lüscher test uses color to build psychological profiles. Each participant puts eight color cards in order of preference, and the result is analyzed to produce the individual's profile. Art therapy is used to help patients express and deal with their personal problems. It places importance on color in understanding feelings. In color application, color is physically placed on the patient, in the form of either colored lights, colored creams, or colored silks.

DOES
MAGIC EXIST?

This bewitching subject means different things to different people. For some, magic is purely a spectacle in which magicians create the illusion of having special powers for a captive audience. However, most people understand that they have not really conjured a rabbit from a hat, cut a woman in half, or made someone disappear in a puff of smoke. Instead, these magicians have learned their trade and practiced their tricks for years in order to perfect their stage performances.

SUPERNATURAL POWERS

Magic in a supernatural sense is another story. In ancient times, there were people considered to be magic makers in Greece, Egypt, and Italy. Society held them in high esteem, believing that these witches and wizards were blessed with supernatural powers. Magic makers would harness the power of nature, recite chants, prepare potions, and carry out spells in order to heal the sick or injured, bring about good luck, or, occasionally, create curses. Many cultures viewed them as wise ones, and they would be summoned to perform their magic to help the wider community by healing health problems and influencing the weather to produce better crops.

WITCH TRIALS

Magic makers did not always prove popular, though. While some religions accepted the belief and use of magic, others rejected it outright as the devil's work on Earth. This came to a head in the 1600s, when the Christian Church decided that magic was satanic, and so magic makers should be punished, tortured, and killed for their craft. Self-appointed witch-hunters traveled across Europe, making wild accusations based on little or no evidence. In 1692, a village called Salem in Massachusetts was the scene of multiple deaths when a group of village girls accused local people of being witches. It resulted in 141 arrests and 20 executions.

TODAY'S MAGIC

Despite the turbulent events of the past, some cultures still believe in magic and encourage its practice. Voodoo (magic of West African origin) and shamanism (witchcraft with a spiritual emphasis) continue today, using a mix of the forces of nature and contact with spirits to make magic. Some tribal communities in parts of Africa keep with tradition and have a shaman (spiritual leader) who is believed to possess magical powers that are used to benefit the whole community. Bubbling cauldrons may no longer be involved, but forms of alternative medicine remain popular, with nature's ingredients used in specific combinations to cure ailments and illnesses. Though it appears in a variety of guises, magic can bring positive changes or, at the very least, add a little bit of sparkle to everyone's lives.

WHAT IS MUSIC?

What sounds like music to your ears could make someone else tune out. As music is not a physical entity, defining it is difficult, especially with all of the genres that have emerged over the past century. If music is simply "organized sound," it could encompass factory noise and washing machines, while the presence of rhythm or harmony can be a question of personal taste. So, while anything may be classed as music, when it's your music, you call the tune.

BACKSTAGE PASS

SOUNDING BOARD
Some artists try to blur the boundaries between art and music, and this is known as sound art. American John Cage (1912–1992) is known for his 1952 composition "4'33'" in which a performer sits onstage for four minutes, 33 seconds. Not a single note is played because Cage wanted the audience to hear the sounds of the environment instead of the performer. He believed that any sounds could be considered music. Does that sound silly to you?

"MUSIC AND RHYTHM FIND THEIR WAY INTO THE SECRET PLACES OF THE SOUL."
Plato (c. 427–347 BCE), Greek philosopher

WHITE NOISE
Another description sometimes given to music is "organized tones." This cannot be the case with rock music, one of the most popular genres in the world. Rock sometimes uses white noise, which has no tone. White noise is sound with continuous frequencies of equal intensity. When advertisements sound louder on television, they are actually not. It is white noise and interference layered in order to attract the audience's attention. White noise makes the brain work harder to understand it, so the viewer unwittingly takes more notice of the advertisements than they otherwise would.

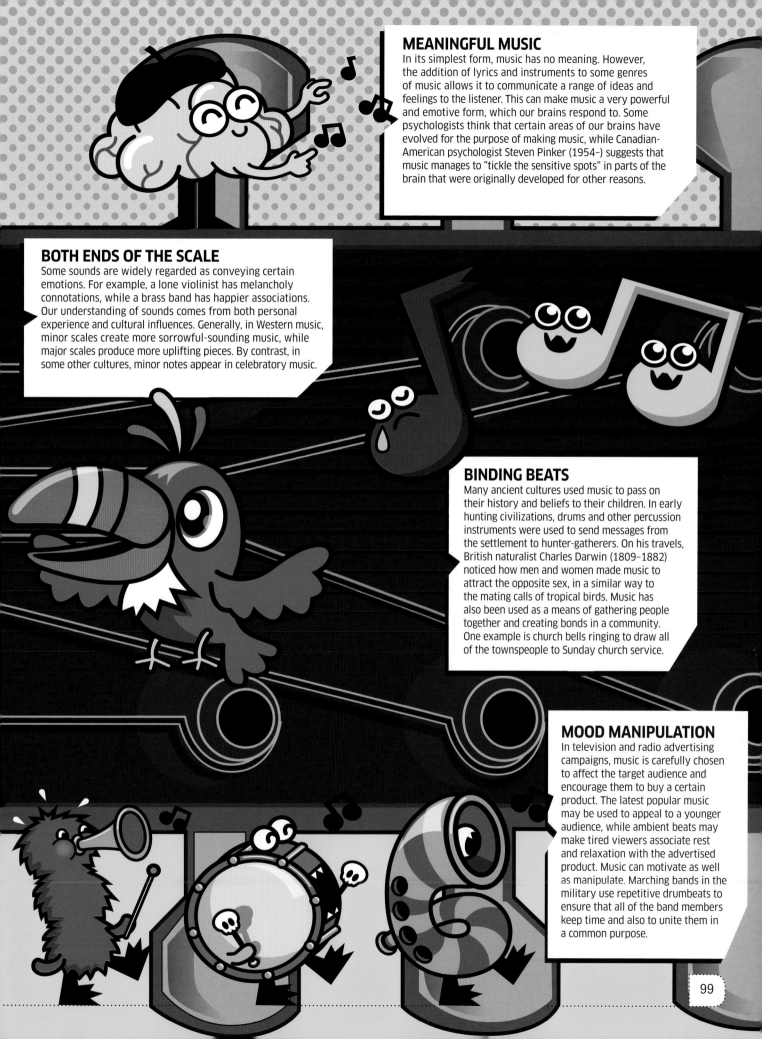

MEANINGFUL MUSIC

In its simplest form, music has no meaning. However, the addition of lyrics and instruments to some genres of music allows it to communicate a range of ideas and feelings to the listener. This can make music a very powerful and emotive form, which our brains respond to. Some psychologists think that certain areas of our brains have evolved for the purpose of making music, while Canadian-American psychologist Steven Pinker (1954–) suggests that music manages to "tickle the sensitive spots" in parts of the brain that were originally developed for other reasons.

BOTH ENDS OF THE SCALE

Some sounds are widely regarded as conveying certain emotions. For example, a lone violinist has melancholy connotations, while a brass band has happier associations. Our understanding of sounds comes from both personal experience and cultural influences. Generally, in Western music, minor scales create more sorrowful-sounding music, while major scales produce more uplifting pieces. By contrast, in some other cultures, minor notes appear in celebratory music.

BINDING BEATS

Many ancient cultures used music to pass on their history and beliefs to their children. In early hunting civilizations, drums and other percussion instruments were used to send messages from the settlement to hunter-gatherers. On his travels, British naturalist Charles Darwin (1809–1882) noticed how men and women made music to attract the opposite sex, in a similar way to the mating calls of tropical birds. Music has also been used as a means of gathering people together and creating bonds in a community. One example is church bells ringing to draw all of the townspeople to Sunday church service.

MOOD MANIPULATION

In television and radio advertising campaigns, music is carefully chosen to affect the target audience and encourage them to buy a certain product. The latest popular music may be used to appeal to a younger audience, while ambient beats may make tired viewers associate rest and relaxation with the advertised product. Music can motivate as well as manipulate. Marching bands in the military use repetitive drumbeats to ensure that all of the band members keep time and also to unite them in a common purpose.

WHY

DO WE NEED TO EXPLORE?

From checking out the next town to exploring the vast expanse of space, people have always boldly gone where no one has gone before. But today's armchair travelers may complain that there are enough problems to fix at home before heading off on a journey into the unknown or that there is nowhere new to discover anyway. But courageous individuals are always ready to take risks by pushing the frontiers of knowledge. So, if we want to be ready to face the future as a forward-thinking, problem-solving, can-do society, we need to explore what's out there.

DOES

EXPLORING IMPROVE KNOWLEDGE?

It most certainly does—anything that helps us know more has got to be good. Exploration is a sure-fire way to discover new things and expand our knowledge. It helps people answer questions that they hadn't even thought of asking. Until European explorers went to North America, no one knew that potatoes existed. By exploring and discovering, we all benefit.

WHAT

ABOUT NEW DISCOVERIES?

They are guaranteed—exploration can introduce or lead us to incredible new discoveries. Consider all of the revolutionary technologies that have appeared as a result of space exploration, such as communication satellites, miniature electronics, smart robots, photovoltaic power, Global Positioning System (GPS), and more.

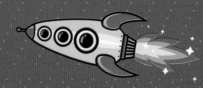

WILL

STAYING IN ONE PLACE GET BORING?

Of course. Very few people stay in one place forever. Exploration gives us the opportunity to discover new habitable worlds. Population growth and limits on food supplies have kept driving us to explore new lands. It would be good to know that there is somewhere else for humankind to go if we are crazy enough to destroy this planet. One scientist says that keeping all of the breeding pairs in one place is no way to run a species. If all of the animals are in one place, a disaster can completely obliterate them. So, avoiding extinction is another great reason to explore!

HOW

DOES EARTH BENEFIT?

Our planet is affected and influenced by external forces. Exploration may help us solve the problems we have on Earth. The more we find out about our planet, the better we will be able to adapt to changes and find solutions to major problems, such as global warming, natural disasters, and overpopulation.

COULD

I BENEFIT, TOO?

Absolutely. We all need to broaden our horizons. The more we know, the more progress we can make on our personal journeys. The idea of exploration may be scary, but the possible benefits are priceless. By challenging ourselves to explore new lands, we expand our minds. It's in our nature to wonder what and where is next. We have imaginations—that's what sets us apart. We need to use them. Go pack your bags . . .

WHERE

TO NEXT?

You decide. But think big. The greatest moments in exploration history have unified and inspired humankind. Think about how many people around the globe marveled at the *Apollo 11* mission to the Moon in 1969. But be sure you pay attention! American astronaut Buzz Aldrin realized that he had missed all of the excitement back on Earth. Upon their return from space, he turned to Neil Armstrong and said, "We missed the whole thing!"

BIOLOGIST BELIEFS

Biology is the study of living things, so biologists certainly have an opinion here. This question has been bugging them since life began (practically), but there are probably as many opinions as there are biologists. Still, they have agreed that there is a sort of "shopping list" of traits common to all living things. Without checking all of these boxes, there is no life. You've checked out.

ENERGY

Living things need to take in a continuous supply of energy in order to function. They use a process called metabolism to access that energy. They need energy to move, grow and repair cells, transport nutrients, and regulate temperature, among other things.

CELLS

All living things require a cell or cells. Cells are the basic ingredients of life, and the smallest units of living matter. Every single living organism on Earth is divided into pieces called cells, each with its own set of functions. There are trillions of cells inside you.

RESPONSIVENESS

Another trait common to living things is responsiveness to their environment. For example, a living thing will respond to a change in sound, heat, light, or contact. Even a simple single-celled critter can detect and move toward light.

REPRODUCTION

A living thing can make a copy of itself through reproduction. Some organisms can reproduce by themselves, which is called asexual reproduction. Others reproduce in pairs—sexual reproduction. They pass their traits to their offspring.

EVOLUTION

Over time, living organisms have the ability to slowly change, or evolve, to better adapt to their environment. They develop ways to cope with their surroundings that their ancestors did not have, so they can live better.

VIRUS ALERT

Although there is plenty of debate, most biologists do not think that viruses are alive. They evolve, have genes, and replicate by making copies of themselves. But viruses are not made of cells (they are little more than a strand of DNA covered with protein), do not have an independent metabolism, and do not take in energy, so they are not considered alive. Even so, they are nothing to sneeze at once they get in your system.

COMPUTER VIRUS

A computer virus is a small piece of rogue software that attaches itself onto real programs and can wreak havoc on a computer. Some people speculate that computer viruses are alive, as they reproduce by attaching to other programs. Although they pass from machine to machine to infect it like a virus spreads between people, they copy themselves exactly, with no possibility of evolution . . . yet. So, a computer virus cannot really be considered alive.

This seems like a silly question. After all, if you are reading this, you must be living, right? We all know what it means to be alive: you move, eat, breathe, go to the supermarket, and so on. Yet it isn't very easy to describe what life itself is, and it is not always easy to tell whether or not something is alive. This question has puzzled philosophers and had scientists scratching their heads for centuries. Let's shop around for an answer. Are you ready to dash to the market?

WHAT IS LIFE ANYWAY?

WASTE REMOVAL

The process of removing waste products from the body is called excretion. Living things must do this because waste can build up in the body and turn poisonous. In humans, waste includes urine, feces, sweat, and carbon dioxide.

GROWTH

All living things grow and develop. They grow by adding new material through a process called mitosis. One cell splits into two separate cells, and then those cells do the same. Development is a change in structure as something gets older.

EXTREMOPHILES

Some organisms survive in conditions that would kill anything else. From frozen lakes to volcanic vents, in dangerous chemical environments to rocks deep inside Earth, these extremophiles are alive and thriving. NASA researchers are especially interested in the microbes that live at very low temperatures. Since it is so cold in space, they might help us figure out if there is life elsewhere in the universe.

DEADHEAD

Some nonliving things may have one or more of these characteristics. For example, ice crystals forming on the edge of a roof can grow into long icicles if the conditions are right, but they are not alive. Biologists divide nonliving things into two groups. In the first group are all of the things that were never part of a living thing, such as a stone. The second group contains all of the things that were once alive, from dinosaur fossils to coal to paper.

ANDROID

Will scientists ever be able to mimic human life? The closest we have come so far is through androids—robots that have been designed to look and act like humans. Scientists have managed to create life-size androids that are capable of walking on two legs, making a range of facial expressions, recognizing speech so that they can converse, and even singing! However, they have not created an android who enjoys doing grocery shopping. Yet.

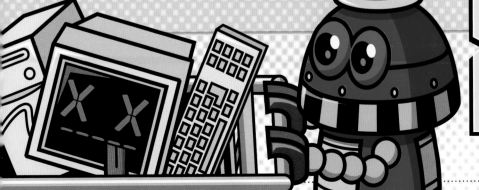

103

CAN COMPUTERS THINK?

The capability of today's computers is truly mind-boggling. Since the world's first electronic versions were turned on less than 100 years ago, computers have made rapid progress and now fulfill a range of functions. Though they may appear to think, computers can only perform tasks that they have been programmed to carry out. Computer behavior and responses cannot match the human brain's thought capacity and complexity . . . yet.

INNER THOUGHTS

Computers can be placed inside robots in an attempt to make them appear more human. Yet the unique inner thoughts experienced by individuals cannot be incorporated into a robot. If thoughts were entered as a program, these would come first from the programmer rather than the computer itself.

ARTIFICIAL INTELLIGENCE

The ability of a computer or machine to perform activities that require thought is known as artificial intelligence. Some people dismiss the notion as irrelevant. After all, if a computer can do its job efficiently, why does it need to think, too? Computer scientists can see the advantages of machines thinking as intelligently as people do. Although programmers strive to find ways of making machines more intelligent, not everyone is convinced. With ideas rooted in science-fiction movies and books, some fear that machines could become self-aware and rise up in rebellion against the people who created them.

FEELINGS

Although it is possible to devise computer programs to imitate generic human thoughts, feelings are even more difficult to recreate. While computers can handle opening a variety of systems at once, they cannot mimic the range of emotions felt by people. Instead, they would have to be ordered (via new programs) to respond in certain ways to user actions.

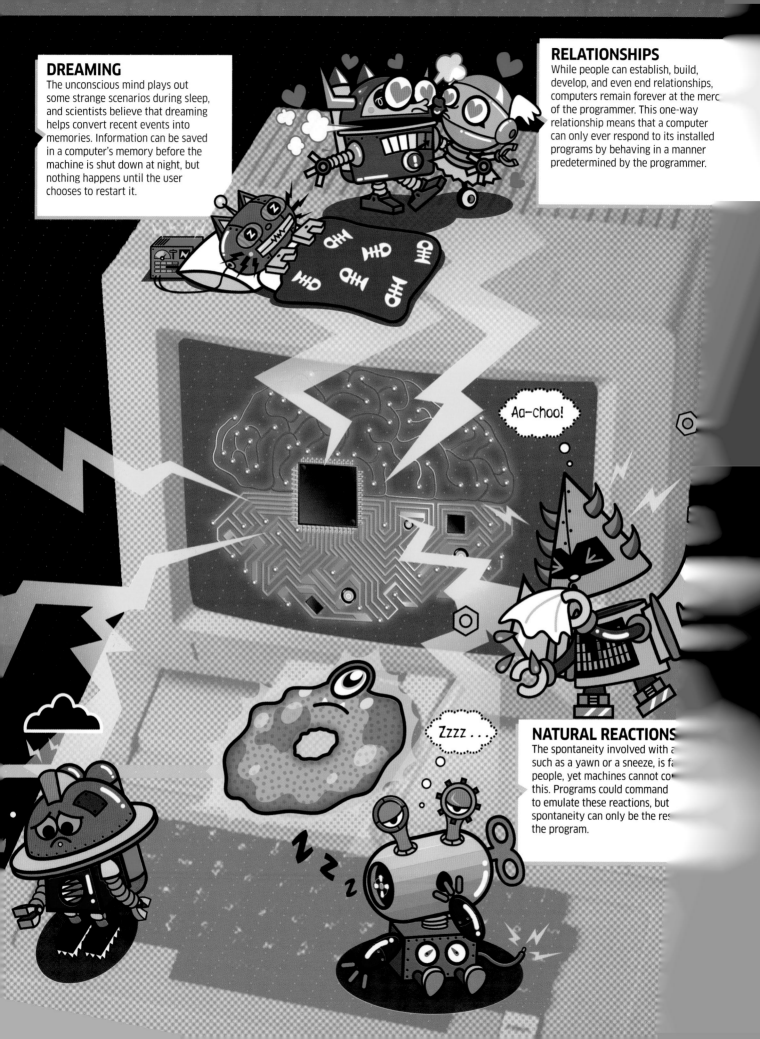

DREAMING
The unconscious mind plays out some strange scenarios during sleep, and scientists believe that dreaming helps convert recent events into memories. Information can be saved in a computer's memory before the machine is shut down at night, but nothing happens until the user chooses to restart it.

RELATIONSHIPS
While people can establish, build, develop, and even end relationships, computers remain forever at the merc of the programmer. This one-way relationship means that a computer can only ever respond to its installed programs by behaving in a manner predetermined by the programmer.

NATURAL REACTIONS
The spontaneity involved with a such as a yawn or a sneeze, is fa people, yet machines cannot co this. Programs could command to emulate these reactions, but spontaneity can only be the res the program.

DO I
NEED TO DO
MATH HOMEWORK?

Do times tables terrify you? Do fractions make you fearful? Does division blur your vision? Are you simply scared of subtraction? Be not afraid, for what your math teachers have been telling you for years is absolutely true: mathematics really is important in our everyday lives. It all adds up to this—without it, we'd be clueless.

WHY MATH MATTERS
Mathematics is a key tool in science. Without it, there would be no physics, chemistry, or astronomy, for example. Math help us get from point A to point B. We depend on math in navigation, aviation, and map-making. In fact, without math, any field that depends on numbers, from architecture to commerce, would fail. We couldn't even get to school in the morning without using math to stay on time. Even in the past, math was essential. It helped the world's greatest empires rise to power.

EGYPTIAN EXPERTS
The ancient Egyptians were excellent at math. They used a decimal system based on ten fingers of the hand, figured out how to multiply and divide with addition and subtraction, and understood concepts such as binary numbers, fractions, and solids. As you might expect from the people who brought you the pyramids, they knew all about triangles. Mathematicians in the ancient world also made key developments in timekeeping. Thanks to the Babylonians, we have 60 seconds in one minute and 60 minutes in one hour, not to mention 360 degrees in a circle.

GREEK GODS
The ancient Greeks were geniuses of geometry, using it to prove that certain mathematical ideas were always true. Top brains including Pythagoras (500s BCE), Aristotle (350s BCE), Euclid (300s BCE), and Archimedes (200s BCE) came up with brilliant theories that you still use in math class today.

OLD CHINA
Mathematics helped the Chinese accomplish amazing feats of engineering , such as the Great Wall. The abacus, attributed to the Chinese, is a device that can add, subtract, multiply, and divide, as well as work with sophisticated mathematical problems such as square roots. The earliest version of the game sudoku appeared in an ancient Chinese text dating back to about 1000 BCE.

INDIAN INFINITY
The decimal and binary number systems were first recorded in Indian math books. The concept of the number zero may have started in India, as well as the understanding of infinity and negative numbers. Between the years 622 and 1600, mathematics flourished in the Islamic world. The mathematicians had ideas way ahead of their time. Algebra, calculus, and trigonometry were developed there.

EUROPEAN EGGHEADS
Key European mathematicians included Leonardo Fibonacci (1200s), who described a number sequence in which each number is the sum of the previous two numbers, René Descartes (1596-1650), who found that curved lines can be described by equations, and Sir Isaac Newton (1643-1727), who made developments in calculus.

OUTNUMBERED
You might not make mathematical history like these legends did, but math is good for your brain. Practicing how to solve mathematical problems boosts your ability to make complex decisions. Learning new math concepts forces you to think in different ways so that your brain can build the connections it needs to solve all kinds of challenges. Now all that's left to say is please go do your math homework!

DO ANIMALS HAVE RIGHTS?

We gather here today to debate the subject of animal rights. Humans often consider the effects they have as a society on the evironment and so on. Understandably, they want to establish whether their actions infringe on the rights of others. But what rights do they have to the animals that live among them? Is it right that they do what they want with animals? Let the debate commence, but without fighting like cats and dogs . . .

COMPANIONS
Humans say that we are their best friends, but some are very cruel to us. We support neutering and spaying so that unwanted animals do not end up in shelters or, worse, being put to sleep. The more exotic creatures among us should not be kept as pets, and humans who breed us should do so with great consideration and care. Owning a pet is not a short-term novelty gift but a long-term rewarding investment.

ANIMAL TESTING
Millions of us are killed, poisoned, or blinded each year in laboratories, testing cosmetic, medical, and household products for humans. We understand that people benefit from animal research—the polio vaccine alone has saved millions of lives. However, there are often reliable alternatives to animal testing, such as computer simulation and human volunteers.

WILDLIFE
Grrreat arguments, thank you. I'll add that hunting wild animals not only kills and injures them, but it also plays with nature's balance. Poaching and smuggling these animals is also an intrusion on their way of life. Hunters may insist that they have a right to kill for food or because it is legal or good for population control, but more responsible action must be taken. Protection programs and conservation projects are the way forward.

WORKING ANIMALS
Animals work hard for humans on farms and as labor. We also entertain you in circuses, races, zoos, rodeos, races, the bullring, and in movies and on television, as well as helping some disabled people. You benefit from our work, so can we not benefit from humane treatment?

PRO ANIMALS
We stand against cruelty toward, and human exploitation of, all animals. We suffer pain and deserve proper and responsible treatment. Humans have a saying they use—do unto others as you would have them do unto you. Practice what you preach! This must surely apply to us creatures, too. It's inhumane to regard us differently. Here are some examples, if it pleases the court . . .

WORST-CASE SCENARIOS

So why are we so eager for these experiments? The new technologies could help us solve a lot of problems, from human health to climate change. In the future, we could design bacteria to soak up carbon dioxide from the atmosphere, provide cheap medicine, or make engine fuel so that we do not rely on coal and oil. Yet critics imagine worst-case scenarios where people hack the technology to create mass-murdering viruses or replicate dinosaur DNA to bring the reptiles roaring back to life.

HUMAN CLONING

Since Dolly the sheep was cloned in 1997, people have bleated on about human cloning. There are two types: therapeutic (cloning cells to use in medical research) and reproductive (making a new you). Positive uses of cloning include providing organs for transplants, allowing infertile or homosexual couples to have a baby, and advancing genetic research. Critics say that cloning will limit gene diversity, which weakens our ability to adapt.

ARTIFICIAL LIFE

In 2010, American biologist Craig Venter (1946–) removed the DNA of a bacterium (a bug that lives on skin) and made copies of it. He then inserted the laboratory-made DNA into the dead "shell" of a different bacterium that had had its DNA removed. The new bacterium started to multiply–a sign of life. Venter's team had created the first living cell controlled completely by "fake" DNA.

STEM CELL RESEARCH

Stem cells can grow into almost any kind of cell. They can replace damaged or dead cells almost anywhere in the body to treat injury or disease. They are harvested from an adult's bone marrow, the umbilical cord in pregnancy, or, controversially, a human embryo in its very early stage (when it consists of about 100 cells). To get the stem cells, the embryo has to be destroyed, and to some people, that is killing a human or destroying a soul–make no bones about it.

CAN
MIRACLES HAPPEN?

Imagine something really amazing happens to you—escaping unscathed from a plane crash, winning a television talent show, or discovering that an unknown uncle has left you a fortune. It would be a significantly life-changing event, and you might describe it as a miracle. Yet these sorts of things are actually the result of chance or coincidence rather than a miracle. The true definition of a miracle is a supernatural happening that cannot be explained in physical terms. Some religious people are certain that these miracles do happen, though there is as yet no scientific proof.

WHAT
ABOUT THE MIRACLES IN THE BIBLE?

For millions of people, the miracles that are described in the Bible, the sacred book of Jews and Christians, really did take place. Others look for alternative explanations. For example, the Bible says that God miraculously parted the waters of the Red Sea to allow the Israelites to flee Egypt. But what if their crossing had coincided with a seismic event, such as a tsunami, that caused the waters to recede? Such a powerful display of nature would have seemed like a miracle.

SO, ARE
PEOPLE CURED BY MIRACLES?

There are many reported cases of people being cured of a disease after praying for a miracle. They believe that God made the disease vanish. But maybe it was the power of their own mind—the belief that they would get better—that brought about their recovery. Or maybe they were getting better anyway. No one knows for sure.

DO
STATUES
PERFORM MIRACLES?

Catholic Christians sometimes report that statues of the Virgin Mary or other saints weep real tears. In 1995, statues of the Hindu god Ganesh, in India, were said to be swallowing milk. Worshipers saw it as a miracle. However, these phenomena can often be explained by physical causes. In the case of Ganesh, the milk was simply being absorbed by capillarity (a process by which liquid rises spontaneously in porous materials) into the stone.

WHAT
ABOUT DISASTER VICTIMS?

In 1985, an earthquake in Mexico City killed more than 10,000 people. Seven days later, 22 newborn babies (known as the "Miracle Babies") were pulled from the rubble alive. Similarly, one victim of the devastating Haiti earthquake in 2010 survived for 28 days before being rescued. To the survivors of such disasters, their families, and rescuers, it is a miracle. In reality, they have just been luckier than all of the others who lost their lives.

WOULD
IT TAKE A MIRACLE TO
WIN THE LOTTERY?

No—someone has to win. But your chances of winning a major national or state lottery are in the millions, as much as 20 million to one in some cases. You are 45 times more likely to be killed by lightning. So, it would certainly seem like a miracle, wouldn't it? Sometimes, when special events happen to one person, they perceive it to be a miracle and forget that it happens to someone else every week. It is a miracle for them personally, but it is not a miracle in the grand scheme of things.

SPEED LIMITS

Imagine that you were in a spaceship traveling near the speed of light, which is much faster than it is possible to go now. When you returned to Earth, all of your friends would be much older. That's not because you hang around old people! It's because time has passed more slowly for you than those you left behind. In a way, you have been a time traveler. Einstein figured out that if we could ever break the speed limit, we could travel through time. Sadly, we're slowpokes and we can't.

BLACK HOLES AND WORMHOLES

Einstein had another theory of general relativity that said that time passes more slowly for objects held in gravitational fields, such as Earth, than for objects far away from the fields. Black holes are areas in space where the gravity is so intense that it sucks in everything, even light and potential time travelers. Black holes could lead to wormholes, tunnels that act as shortcuts through space and time. Hole-y moley!

EINSTEIN'S THEORY

In his famous theory of relativity, big-thinking German physicist Albert Einstein (1879–1955) proposed that space and time are aspects of the same thing: space-time. There is a speed limit of precisely 186,282 miles (299,792 km) per second for anything that travels through space-time. Light always obeys the rules and travels through empty space at the speed limit. Einstein deduced that you need to travel faster than light to travel through space-time.

LAWS OF PHYSICS

In 1895, English author H. G. Wells (1866–1946) wrote a book called *The Time Machine* about a vehicle that could take people through time. It might sound far-fetched, but physicists have a saying—if nothing is prohibited, it must happen at some point. There is nothing in the laws of physics that prohibits time travel. The prospect of travel into the future seems possible, because time passes at a different rate in orbit than it does on the ground. Even though there are no laws to prohibit travel into the past, most physicists agree that it is probably less likely to happen.

> "ONCE CONFINED TO FANTASY AND SCIENCE FICTION, TIME TRAVEL IS NOW SIMPLY AN ENGINEERING PROBLEM."
> Michio Kaku (1947–), American physicist

IS TIME TRAVEL A POSSIBILITY?

We all travel in time, at the rate of one hour per hour. Duh! But could we travel faster or slower than that? Could it be possible to travel backward and forward in time? Think what a difference that would make. If you have homework due tomorrow, how about going back in time two days so that you have more time to finish it, then zipping forward to the present

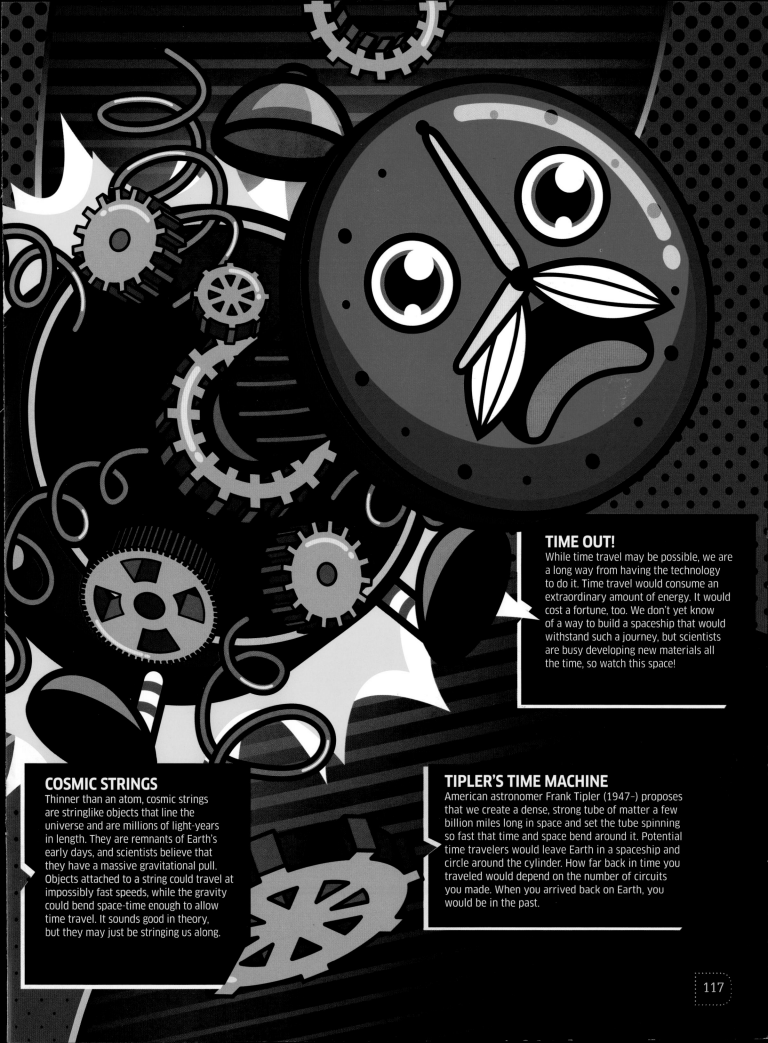

TIME OUT!

While time travel may be possible, we are a long way from having the technology to do it. Time travel would consume an extraordinary amount of energy. It would cost a fortune, too. We don't yet know of a way to build a spaceship that would withstand such a journey, but scientists are busy developing new materials all the time, so watch this space!

COSMIC STRINGS

Thinner than an atom, cosmic strings are stringlike objects that line the universe and are millions of light-years in length. They are remnants of Earth's early days, and scientists believe that they have a massive gravitational pull. Objects attached to a string could travel at impossibly fast speeds, while the gravity could bend space-time enough to allow time travel. It sounds good in theory, but they may just be stringing us along.

TIPLER'S TIME MACHINE

American astronomer Frank Tipler (1947–) proposes that we create a dense, strong tube of matter a few billion miles long in space and set the tube spinning so fast that time and space bend around it. Potential time travelers would leave Earth in a spaceship and circle around the cylinder. How far back in time you traveled would depend on the number of circuits you made. When you arrived back on Earth, you would be in the past.

CAN YOU STEP IN THE SAME RIVER TWICE?

An ancient Greek philosopher named Heraclitus (535-475 BCE) first asked himself the question about 2,500 years ago and came up with this response, "You could not step twice into the same river; for other waters are ever flowing onto you." The water in the river is always rushing forward, so although it looks the same, by the time you place your foot in the river on a second occasion, it is different. Of course, you could answer the question another way. Even though the water is always changing, the river itself remains the same—the Thames is always called the Thames, the Mississippi remains the Mississippi, and the Ganges is still the Ganges. In this sense, you can step in the same river as many times as you like, but it is not the same water wetting your feet each time.

CONSTANT CHANGE

Heraclitus was making a point about change. He believed that everything is always changing, and he was right. For example, the cells in our bodies are replaced countless times during our lifetime. If they did not, our bodies could not grow and function. Yet we remain the same person at all stages of our life, whether a baby, teenager, or senior citizen. Similarly, we live on a restless (dynamic) planet. Even an object as apparently fixed and unchangeable as rock is always on the move. Molten rock (magma) makes its way through cracks in Earth's crust, where it cools and solidifies to form granite rocks. Wind and rain erodes the rocks, and they are washed into rivers as gravel and sand before ending up on the seabed. Earth's crust is divided into huge floating plates. When they collide into one another, layers of rock push up to form mountain ranges. Around 30 million years ago, India crashed into Asia to form the Himalaya Mountains, and it is still moving north at a rate of 2 in. (5 cm) per year. That's twice as fast as human fingernails, which grow about 0.9 in. (2.3 cm) per year.

WATER RECYCLING

Water (H_2O) can change its state from a liquid to a solid (ice) or a gas (vapor) without altering its molecular structure. Most of the water on Earth probably erupted from volcanoes about four billion years ago, collecting as vapor in the atmosphere. Water is continually being moved around the planet. The Sun's heat turns water from the oceans into vapor, which rises into the air, where it cools and forms clouds made of tiny water droplets. Winds blow the clouds across the land, and they release their moisture as rain or snow to fill lakes and rivers that drain into the oceans. This brings us back to the river you stepped in earlier. In the words of American philosopher Ralph Waldo Emerson (1803-1882), "We change, whether we like it or not."

"All is flux; nothing stays still." Heraclitus (535-475 BCE)

GLOSSARY

ABDUCTION
The criminal act of capturing and taking someone away against their will.

AGNOSTIC
Someone who neither believes or disbelieves in the existence of God.

ALIEN
A being from outer space.

AMBIVERT
A person whose character consists of a mix of introverted and extroverted qualities.

ANDROID
A robot with the form, characteristics, or behavior of a human.

ASTEROID
A small rocky body that orbits the sun.

ASTRONOMER
A person who studies the stars, planets, and other objects in space.

ATHEIST
Someone who does not believe in the existence of God.

BACTERIA
A group of single-celled microorganisms, some of which are harmless, but some can cause disease in people.

BIG BANG
The hugely explosive event that marked the beginning of the universe 13.7 billion years ago.

BINARY
A two-digit (0 and 1) number system used by computers to store data.

BRAINWASHING
The use of psychological games in an effort to instill certain ideas and beliefs in a person.

CAPITALISM
An economic system based on private ownership of the means of production, distribution, and exchange.

CLUSTER
A group of galaxies or stars held together by gravity.

COMMUNISM
A system of government in which the state controls the economy, and goods are equally shared by people.

CREATIONISM
The religious belief that all life, Earth, and the universe were created by a supernatural being.

DARK ENERGY
An energy form that makes up 73 per cent of the universe and that is responsible for the expansion of the universe.

DARK MATTER
Matter that does not emit energy but whose gravity affects its surroundings.

DEMOCRACY
A government elected by the people.

DINOSAUR
Any of the many now-extinct terrestrial reptiles from the Mesozoic era (about 250 million years ago to about 65 million years ago).

DNA
Deoxyribonucleic acid (DNA) is the hereditary material in humans and most other organisms.

ECOSYSTEM
A system formed by the interaction of a community of organisms within their environment.

ENDORPHIN
Any of several substances secreted in the brain that have a pain-relieving effect on the body.

EVOLUTION
A gradual process in which something changes into a different and often more complex or effective form.

FOSSIL
The remains of a plant or animal from a past geological age, embedded and preserved in Earth's crust.

GALAXY
A vast group of stars, gas, and dust held together by the forces of gravity.

GENE
A hereditary unit consisting of a sequence of DNA.

GENETICS
The branch of biology that studies heredity and variation between organisms.

GENOCIDE
The intentional killing of a racial or cultural group.

GLOBAL WARMING
An increase in global average surface temperature as a result of climate change.

GRAVITY
A force of attraction found throughout the universe.

HALLOWEEN
A celebration on October 31, the evening before All Saints' Day, in which children wear scary outfits and play practical jokes.

HIBERNATION
The dormant, or resting, state in which some animals spend the winter.

HIEROGLYPHICS
A writing system of picture symbols used in ancient Egypt.

HYPNOSIS
A sleeplike condition induced by slow voices or movements. Under hypnosis, people often respond to questions that they might not normally answer.

IMMUNE SYSTEM
The group of organs, tissues, and cells that works together to protect the human body from disease and infection.

LIGHT-YEAR
A unit of distance. One light-year (ly) is the distance that light travels in one year.

LINGUISTICS
The scientific study of language.

MAGIC
The craft of using charms, spells, and rituals that are believed to have supernatural powers in order to control natural forces.

MATRIARCH
A female who rules a family, clan, or tribe.

MATTER
The substance of which things are made.

MENTAL ILLNESS
A psychological state that causes distress or disability.

MORALITY
Beliefs based on the principles of what is right and wrong.

ORATOR
An eloquent and experienced public speaker.

ORGANISM
An individual member of a biological species.

PAGODA
A multi-story temple or other religious building, usually found in the Far East.

PALEONTOLOGIST
A scientist who studies prehistoric life, especially fossils.

PATRIARCH
A male who rules a family, clan, or tribe.

PICTOGRAM
A symbol in the form of a picture that is supposed to represent an object or concept.

PREDATOR
An animal that survives by hunting and eating other animals.

REINCARNATION
The rebirth of the soul in another body or form after death.

SCIENTIST
An expert who adopts scientific principles to pursue a natural or physical science.

SKEPTIC
A person who routinely doubts beliefs and ideas held by many.

SOLAR SYSTEM
The Sun and the objects that orbit it, including the planets and smaller bodies.

SOUL MATE
One of two people deeply compatible with each other.

SUPERNATURAL
Anything that cannot be explained by science or logic.

SUPERNOVA
A massive star that explodes, leaving material behind.

TELEPATHY
The idea that people can directly communicate thoughts and emotions from one mind to another without using the five basic senses.

UFO
Meaning unidentified flying object, this mysterious flying shape cannot always be explained, and some people insist that it is an alien spacecraft.

UNIVERSE
Everything that exists.

INDEX

CREDITS

Dorling Kindersley would like to thank Mike and Katie at TADO for their illustrations,
Stephanie Pliakas for proofreading, and Jackie Brind for the index.
In addition, thanks goes to Millie Popovic for design and editorial assistance.

The publisher would like to thank the following for their kind permission to
reproduce their photographs:

(Key: b–below/bottom; c–center)
Alamy Images: Art Directors & TRIP/Helene Rogers 104b. **Corbis:** Lawrence Manning 105cb;
mood board 8–9. **Dorling Kindersley:** Luminis/Dreamstime 70–71b. **Getty Images:** Stone/Dan
Saelinger 102–103. **iStockphoto.com:** T-Immagini 105c. **Science Photo Library:** Volker Steger 105.

All other images © Dorling Kindersley

For further information, see www.dkimages.com

"MY GRANDFATHER ONCE TOLD ME THAT THERE WERE TWO KINDS OF PEOPLE:
THOSE WHO DO THE WORK AND THOSE WHO TAKE THE CREDIT. HE TOLD ME
TO TRY TO BE IN THE FIRST GROUP; THERE WAS MUCH LESS COMPETITION."

Indira Gandhi (1917–1984),
prime minister of India